HOW TO EMBRACE YOUR SPARK

HOW TO EMBRACE YOUR SPARK

A SELF-LOVE GUIDE FOR TEEN GIRLS TO BUILD CONFIDENCE, BOOST SELF-ESTEEM AND PRACTICE SELF-CARE

TEEN GIRL GUIDES

ELLA BRADLEY

Copyright © 2024 by Ella Bradley

All rights reserved. No part of this book may be reproduced, stored in a retrieval system, or transmitted in any form or by any means, electronic, mechanical, photocopying, recording, or otherwise, without the prior written permission of the publisher, Teilingen Press.

The information contained in this book is based on the author's personal experiences and research. While every effort has been made to ensure the accuracy of the information presented, the author and publisher cannot be held responsible for any errors or omissions.

This book is intended for general informational purposes only and is not a substitute for professional medical, legal, or financial advice. If you have specific questions about any medical, legal, or financial matters matters, you should consult with a qualified healthcare professional, attorney, or financial advisor.

Teilingen Press is not affiliated with any product or vendor mentioned in this book. The views expressed in this book are those of the author and do not necessarily reflect the views of Teilingen Press.

For my beautiful daughters.

Let your light shine. Shine within you so that it can shine on someone else.

OPRAH WINFREY

CONTENTS

Embracing Your Spark — xiii

1. DISCOVERING WHO YOU ARE — 1
   Your Values and Beliefs — 3
   Your Strengths and Talents — 4
   Embracing Your Quirks — 5
   Realizing Your Dreams — 7
   Chapter Summary — 8

2. CULTIVATING POSITIVE SELF-TALK — 11
   How to Challenge Negative Thoughts — 13
   The Power of Affirmations — 14
   How to Create a Positive Mindset — 16
   The Power of Gratitude — 17
   Case Study: Lily's Transformation Through Positive Self-Talk and Gratitude — 19
   Chapter Summary — 21

3. BUILDING HEALTHY RELATIONSHIPS — 23
   Understanding Boundaries and Respect — 25
   How to Navigate Friendships — 26
   How to Deal with Conflict — 28
   Self-Love in Relationships — 30
   Case Study: Emma's Journey to Self-Respect and Healthy Friendships — 31
   Chapter Summary — 32

4. EMBRACING YOUR BODY — 35
   Celebrating Diversity — 37
   Building Healthy Habits — 38
   How to Deal with Body Shaming — 39
   Case Study: Mia's Path to Body Positivity and Self-Love — 41
   Chapter Summary — 42

5. FINDING YOUR CREATIVE SIDE — 45
- How to Overcome Creative Blocks — 47
- How to Set Goals for Your Projects — 48
- The Role of Discipline — 50
- Celebrating Your Achievements — 51
- Chapter Summary — 52

6. MANAGING STRESS AND ANXIETY — 55
- Mindfulness and Relaxation Techniques — 57
- The Importance of Self-Care — 59
- How to Set Healthy Boundaries — 61
- Seeking Support When Needed — 64
- Case Study: Alex's Journey Through Stress and Self-Discovery — 65
- Chapter Summary — 67

7. THE POWER OF RESILIENCE — 69
- How to Build a Resilient Mindset — 70
- Overcoming Obstacles — 72
- Learning from Failure — 73
- How to Stay Motivated — 74
- Chapter Summary — 76

8. EXPLORING SPIRITUALITY AND INNER PEACE — 77
- Finding Your Spiritual Path — 78
- Practices for Inner Peace — 79
- The Role of Nature and Solitude — 81
- Connecting with a Higher Power — 82
- Case Study: Zoe's Quest for Inner Peace and Spiritual Connection — 83
- Chapter Summary — 85

9. SPEAKING UP — 87
- The Power of No — 89
- Advocating for Yourself and Others — 90
- Public Speaking and Communication Skills — 91
- Leaving a Legacy — 92
- Chapter Summary — 94

10. NAVIGATING CHANGE	95
Embracing New Beginnings	97
How to Deal with Loss and Grief	98
The Role of Support Systems	100
Looking Forward with Hope	101
Chapter Summary	103
Your Self-Love Journey	105
Your Feedback Matters	111
About the Author	113
Also by Ella Bradley	115

EMBRACING YOUR SPARK

Welcome to the beginning of a journey that is entirely your own. This is a journey of discovery, growth, and, most importantly, love—the kind of love that starts with you. It's a path you're not meant to walk alone, but rather, one shared with the wisdom of those who've walked it before and the friendship of those who walk it alongside you.

In the following chapters, we will explore the concept of self-love. Self-love might seem broad and sometimes cliched, but it is as important to your well-being as the air you breathe. Self-love is the basis upon which you build your dreams, the armor that protects you when you doubt yourself, and the light that guides you back home to yourself when the world seems dark.

Loving yourself helps you see what's special about you, empowering you to shine and embrace your individual spark.

Self-love isn't about perfection. It's not a destination you arrive at, declaring victory. Instead, it's about embracing every part of yourself—your strengths, vulnerabilities, successes, and setbacks.

It's about recognizing your worth and value, free from the opinions and thoughts of others.

This journey is about learning to be your best friend, top supporter, and most trusted adviser. It's about setting boundaries that make you happy, pursuing passions you care about, and making choices that reflect your love for yourself.

As we explore the different elements of self-love, know that this journey is uniquely yours. Your path may twist and turn, rise and fall, in ways different from anyone else's. And that's okay. In fact, it's more than okay—it's beautiful. Because it's by navigating these personal experiences that you'll discover your strength and the boundless capacity of your heart to love.

So, take a deep breath and step forward with courage and curiosity. You are about to embark on one of the most important adventures of your life—the journey of loving and celebrating the incredible person that you are.

WHAT IS SELF-LOVE?

Self-love, in simple terms, is a deep acceptance and appreciation of oneself. It's about recognizing your worth, embracing your uniqueness, and nurturing your well-being. It's a journey of understanding that you are enough, just as you are, without needing to prove anything to anyone else. Self-love is not just about feeling good about yourself—it's about treating yourself with kindness, respect, and compassion, especially when you might feel you don't deserve it.

Self-love is a powerful act of defiance in a world that often tries to tell you how to act, look, and dream. It's choosing to honor your feelings, listen to your inner voice, and set boundaries that protect yourself. It's about making choices that reflect what you want rather than what others expect of you.

Self-love is also about recognizing that you are a work in progress and that growth and mistakes are part of the journey. It's understanding that you don't have to be perfect to be worthy of love—especially your own. This means forgiving yourself when you stumble and knowing that every day is a new opportunity to treat yourself better.

Self-love involves taking care of your physical, emotional, and mental health. It's about making time for activities that nourish your soul. It's also about surrounding yourself with people who uplift you and letting go of relationships that drain your energy.

At its core, self-love helps you build an authentic and fulfilling life. It's the light that guides you back to yourself when the world tries to pull you away. While the path to self-love may look different for everyone, the destination is the same: a place of inner peace, strength, and joy.

As you embark on this journey, remember that self-love is not a destination but a practice. It's something you cultivate every day in your choices and how you treat yourself. And though the journey may not always be easy, every step you take towards loving yourself more is a step towards living a more authentic, happy life.

WHY SELF-LOVE MATTERS

In the tapestry of life, each thread represents a unique aspect of who we are, weaving together to form the intricate masterpiece that is you. You control your life, deciding which threads to weave in and which to leave out. It's a time of exploration, of discovering who you are and who you want to become.

Self-love is not just a trendy term; it's the basis upon which you build your sense of self-worth and confidence. But why does it matter so much, especially for you, at this moment in your life?

During your teenage years, you face many pressures, from academic expectations to social conflicts. The world around you seems to be constantly shifting, and with it, the idea of who you're supposed to be. It's easy to get lost in the noise, compare yourself to others, and feel like you're not good enough. This is where self-love steps in as a powerful tool.

Embracing self-love means allowing yourself to be imperfect, make mistakes, and learn from them. It means putting yourself first and prioritizing your mental and physical well-being. When you love yourself, you acknowledge your strengths and weaknesses and accept them as integral parts of your identity. This is the starting point for growth and self-improvement.

Self-love also influences how you interact with the world. It teaches you to value your own opinions and stand up for yourself. It empowers you to follow your own path, rather than one set by societal expectations or peer pressure. When you love yourself, you express confidence and authenticity, attracting positive relationships and experiences into your life.

Perhaps most importantly, self-love sets the tone for how you allow others to treat you. It instills a sense of self-respect that demands the same from those around you. By valuing yourself, you teach others to value you, too. This doesn't mean you won't face rejection or criticism. Still, it means that you'll have the tools to handle it, knowing that the opinions of others don't determine your worth.

Self-love is not just about feeling good in the moment; it's about building a resilient, compassionate, and authentic self that can navigate the complexities of life with grace and strength. It's about recognizing that you are enough, exactly as you are, and that you deserve to be loved, first and foremost, by yourself.

THE MYTHS OF SELF-LOVE

In a world where you're growing and finding your place, self-love is a term you've probably heard over a thousand times. It's praised as the key to happiness, the solution to life's challenges, and the gateway to fulfillment. But as we peel back the layers of what self-love truly means, let's debunk some of the myths that might be holding you back from fully embracing and understanding it.

Loving Yourself Is Selfish

Firstly, there's a common misconception that self-love comes with selfishness. This couldn't be further from the truth. Loving yourself doesn't mean you disregard the feelings or needs of others. It means you recognize your worth, understanding that you can't pour from an empty cup. When you take care of yourself, you're better positioned to care for and empathize with others.

Self-Love Is All About Treating Yourself

Another myth is that self-love is all about pampering yourself with material things or experiences. While treating yourself can be a part of self-care, self-love is much deeper than that. It's about the internal conversations you have with yourself, the ability to forgive yourself for mistakes, and the commitment to support your growth and happiness. It's not just about feeling good in the moment but having respect towards yourself that carries you through life's ups and downs.

Self-Love Is a Destination

There's also a belief that self-love is a destination—a point you reach where you're entirely content and free from self-doubt or criticism. The truth is that self-love is a journey, not a fixed state. It's normal to have days when you don't love yourself. What matters is the ongoing effort to treat yourself compassionately, recognizing that you are a work in progress.

Self-Love Is Conditional

Lastly, the idea that self-love can only be achieved once you've reached certain milestones or look a certain way is a myth. Your worth is not dependent on your achievements, appearance, or any external factors. Self-love starts from within, from an acceptance of who you are at this moment.

By debunking these myths, we pave the way for a more genuine and empowering understanding of self-love. It's not about perfection or external validation but about embracing your unique journey, with all its imperfections, and treating yourself with the same kindness you'd offer to someone you love deeply.

Let's now explore how to lay the groundwork for deep self-love, setting the stage for growth, resilience, and a happier life.

HOW TO LET YOUR SELF-LOVE GROW

Understanding and debunking the myths that surround self-love is just the beginning. Now, we pivot towards laying down the foundation upon which your self-love can grow and flourish. This foundation is not made from the external validations or achievements that society often tells us to chase. Instead, it is built from the inside out, starting with the core of who you are.

Self-Awareness

Let's begin with self-awareness. Self-awareness goes hand-in-hand with self-love. It involves taking a deep, honest look at yourself — your thoughts, feelings, motivations, and behaviors. It's about recognizing your strengths and accepting your weaknesses without judgment. This process isn't always easy. It requires courage to face yourself and acknowledge the parts of you that you might wish to change.

Self-Compassion

Once you've started practicing self-awareness, the next step is to practice self-compassion. Imagine speaking to yourself as you would to a close friend. You wouldn't criticize a friend for making a mistake or not being perfect, so why do it to yourself? Self-compassion means being kind and understanding when you fail or confront your personal flaws. Imperfection is part of the human experience, and everyone experiences it at some point in their lives.

Setting Boundaries

Setting boundaries is another crucial element of your foundation. Boundaries help protect your energy and emotional well-being. They are the guidelines you set for how you want to be treated by others and how you treat yourself. This might mean learning to say no, prioritizing your needs, or distancing yourself from toxic relationships. We will explore boundaries in more detail in later chapters.

Gratitude

Lastly, gratitude plays a significant role in the building of self-love. Gratitude shifts your focus from what you are missing to what is already in your life. It's about appreciating the small victories, the beauty in the every day, and the lessons learned from challenges. By practicing gratitude, you encourage a positive mindset that supports growth and self-love. We'll explore gratitude in more detail later on in the book.

Building a strong foundation for self-love is an ongoing process. It doesn't happen overnight, and there will be setbacks. But with each step you take — through self-awareness, self-compassion, setting boundaries, and practicing gratitude — you are laying down the stones on your path toward a deeper, more fulfilling relationship with yourself. This is your journey, unique and beautiful, and it's all about becoming the best version of yourself, one step at a time.

CHAPTER SUMMARY

- Self-love is a journey of discovery, growth, and acceptance that is important for one's personal well-being and fulfillment.
- Self-love involves embracing all aspects of yourself, including your strengths, weaknesses, successes, and setbacks, and recognizing your worth.
- The journey of self-love involves learning to be your own best friend, setting boundaries that honor well-being, and making choices that reflect self-love.
- Self-love is important for teenage girls, as it builds a sense of self-worth and confidence, especially during their adolescent years, which are filled with challenges and pressures.
- Several myths about self-love include the misconceptions that self-love is selfish, materialistic, a fixed destination, or depending on your achievements or appearance.
- Self-awareness, self-compassion, setting boundaries, and practicing gratitude can help lay the foundation for growth in self-love, emphasizing the process and journey over perfection.

CHAPTER 1
DISCOVERING WHO YOU ARE

One of the most exciting paths in the journey of discovering who you are is exploring your unique self. This exploration is not about fitting into predefined molds or meeting society's expectations. It's about uncovering who you really are—your passions, quirks, strengths, and even your struggles. It's about embracing every part of yourself with love and compassion.

Your uniqueness is your superpower. It's what sets you apart from everyone else in the world. Think about it—out of billions of people, there is only one you. You have a combination of talents, thoughts, feelings, and experiences that nobody else has. This uniqueness is not something to shy away from; it's something to celebrate!

To start embracing your unique self, acknowledge and accept your feelings and thoughts as valid. It's okay to feel deeply, have opinions, and see the world differently. Your perspective adds valuable color to the canvas of life.

Consider your strengths and weaknesses honestly. Everyone has both, and recognizing them is not about judging yourself but about getting to know yourself better. Your strengths are your gifts to the world, while your weaknesses are opportunities to learn and improve.

Your understanding of yourself will change as you grow. Be patient and kind to yourself through this process. Celebrate your wins, learn from your setbacks, and always remember you are in charge of self-love.

By celebrating your unique self, you're supporting your well-being and setting a powerful example for others. You're showing the world that it's okay to be different, follow your own path, and love yourself every step of the way.

In the next section, we'll delve deeper into what shapes us—our values and beliefs. These guiding principles influence our thoughts, decisions, and actions. Understanding your values and beliefs is crucial for living authentically and fostering a true sense of self-love.

YOUR VALUES AND BELIEFS

Understanding your values and beliefs is like uncovering the compass that guides your heart and soul. These silent whispers steer you through life's many paths, helping you decide what feels right and doesn't align with your life.

Values and beliefs are the colors with which you paint your world. They influence your decisions, shape your dreams, and mold your reactions to the world around you. They are deeply personal, often inherited from the people you love, and uniquely yours to embrace or question as you grow older.

Imagine your values as seeds planted within you. With proper care, these seeds grow into strong trees that provide shelter and direction throughout your life. These values might include honesty, loyalty, and self-compassion—qualities that resonate with who you want to be.

On the other hand, beliefs are the narratives we hold about the world, ourselves, and our place within it. They can be empowering, telling us we are capable and deserving of love, or limiting, holding us back with doubts and fears. We must examine these beliefs and ask ourselves if they truly serve us or need to be gently released.

Discovering your values and beliefs takes time and effort. It's a journey that involves turning inward, being curious, and sometimes, having the courage to challenge what you've always thought to be true. It's about asking yourself the hard questions: What matters most to me? Why do I believe what I believe? How do these beliefs shape my view of myself and the world?

Your values and beliefs are allowed to evolve. As you grow and change, so too can your understanding of what matters most. This is not a sign of inconsistency but of growth. Embrace this evolution because it shows your commitment to becoming the most authentic version of yourself.

When you embrace your values and beliefs, you can live a life with more purpose and passion. You can navigate life's challenges gracefully and confidently. You learn to make choices that align with your deepest truths, leading to a sense of inner peace.

Your values and beliefs are the roots from which your strengths and talents blossom. They shape not just the person you are today but the incredible person you are becoming. Welcome this journey of discovery, because when you understand your values and beliefs, you unlock the full potential of your unique, beautiful self.

YOUR STRENGTHS AND TALENTS

Recognizing and embracing your strengths and talents is like uncovering hidden treasures within yourself. Each of us is a unique blend of abilities and gifts, and finding what you naturally excel at is empowering and a fundamental step toward building self-love.

Think of your strengths as your personal superpowers. These could range from being a good listener, having a knack for solving puzzles, and expressing yourself creatively through art, music, or writing.

Your talents, on the other hand, are the skills you've practiced or are naturally good at. You may have a green thumb, a gift for storytelling, or an exceptional ability in sports. These strengths and talents contribute to who you are, and acknowledging them helps you appreciate your uniqueness.

Discovering your strengths and talents might require some reflection. Start by reflecting on activities that bring you joy or tasks you find fulfilling. Often, our strengths are intertwined with our passions. Ask yourself, what are the things you do that make time fly? What are the tasks that people often come to you for help with? The answers to these questions are clues to your inherent strengths and talents.

It's also beneficial to seek feedback from those who know you well. Sometimes, others can see the brilliance in us that we might overlook. Friends, family members, and teachers can offer insights into your abilities and talents. However, remember, the aim is not to compare yourself with others but to understand and celebrate your skills.

Once you've identified your strengths and talents, the next step is to develop them. This could mean taking up new hobbies, joining clubs or teams that align with your interests, or simply dedicating time to practice and improve. Embracing and developing your talents boosts your self-esteem and opens up opportunities for personal growth and satisfaction.

Your strengths and talents are a significant part of what makes you unique. They are tools for achieving success and ways to find joy and purpose in life.

As you continue to explore and understand yourself, remember that your quirks are also integral to your identity. They add depth to your character and make you who you are. Embracing these aspects of yourself is as important as recognizing your strengths and talents.

EMBRACING YOUR QUIRKS

After thinking about your strengths and talents, it's time to turn our attention to something equally important and delightful— your quirks. These are the unique traits and habits that make you, well, you. They might be the things you've been teased about, or perhaps you've tried to hide them, thinking they make you stand out too much. But here's a secret: those very quirks make you unforgettable and irreplaceably you.

Embracing your quirks is like giving yourself a big, warm hug. It acknowledges that even the parts of you that don't fit into typical boxes are worthy of love and celebration. Think about the people you admire most; aren't their quirks what make them stand out? The way they laugh, the passions they pursue, or even the unique way they see the world—these are the things that draw us to them.

Your quirks could be anything from a passion for collecting something unusual to an eccentric fashion sense, a unique way of expressing yourself, or even an uncommon hobby. Whatever it is, it reflects your inner world, creativity, and perspective on life. Embracing these aspects of yourself can be a powerful step toward loving who you are.

But how do you start embracing these quirks, especially if you've spent years trying to cover them up? Begin by acknowledging them. Write them down, talk about them, or express them in any way you can. Then, try to understand why you felt the need to hide them. Often, it's because we fear judgment or rejection. But remember, anyone who doesn't appreciate the real you isn't someone whose opinion should matter to you.

Next, celebrate your quirks. Wear that quirky outfit with pride, dive into your unusual hobbies, and let your unique light shine brightly. The more you do it, the more you'll find people who love and appreciate you for who you truly are—quirks and all. These are the people who matter. These are the connections that will enrich your life.

Some days, you'll feel bold and unapologetic. On other days, you might feel the urge to retreat. That's okay. Self-love and acceptance are practices that take time. As you continue to embrace your quirks, you'll find that they are not just things to be tolerated but celebrated. They are the essence of your individuality, the signature of your soul. And in a world that often tries to fit us into neatly labeled boxes, choosing to love every part of yourself is a radical act of self-love.

So, let's not just dream about a future where we're fully accepted. Let's create it, starting with accepting and loving ourselves, quirks and all.

REALIZING YOUR DREAMS

After embracing your quirks, it's time to delve deeper into the essence of who you are and who you aspire to be. This journey of self-discovery is not just about recognizing your unique traits but also about discovering your dreams. Dreams are sparks for your future, ignited in your imagination and fueled by your hopes and aspirations.

Dreams hold immense power. They are not just fantasies or fleeting thoughts that pass through your mind. They reflect your innermost desires and potential. When you dream, you allow yourself to picture a life beyond your current reality. You open up to the possibilities of achieving greatness, experiencing joy, and impacting the world.

The path to realizing your dreams is not always straightforward. It requires courage, perseverance, and self-belief. There will be moments of doubt and fear when your dreams seem too distant or challenging to achieve. This is where self-love comes into play. Loving yourself means believing in your ability to overcome obstacles and reach for the stars, even when others might doubt you.

To harness the power of your dreams, start by permitting yourself to dream big. Allow your imagination to run wild without criticism or judgment. Write down your dreams, no matter how grand or silly they may seem. Visualizing your dreams can make them more concrete and achievable.

Next, take actionable steps toward your dreams. Break them down into smaller, manageable goals. Celebrate each progression, no matter how small, as it brings you one step closer to your dream. Remember, the journey toward your dreams is as important as the destination. It is a journey of growth, learning, and self-discovery.

Surround yourself with positivity and support. Seek mentors and role models who inspire and believe in your potential. Their guidance and encouragement can be invaluable as you navigate the challenges and setbacks that may arise.

Lastly, never lose sight of the essence of who you are. Your dreams are a reflection of your unique spirit and potential. Embrace them with open arms and a loving heart. Believe in yourself and your ability to make your dreams a reality. The power of dreams is limitless, and so is your potential to achieve them.

CHAPTER SUMMARY

- Discovering your unique self involves embracing your passions, quirks, strengths, and weaknesses and celebrating what sets you apart.

- Acknowledging and accepting your feelings and thoughts as valid is important in embracing your uniqueness.
- Exploring your interests and what you love doing can provide clues to your passions, contributing to your unique identity.
- Recognizing your strengths and weaknesses allows for personal growth and a better understanding of yourself.
- Embracing your unique self is a lifelong journey that involves patience, self-love, and acceptance, setting a powerful example for others.
- Understanding and aligning with your values and beliefs is essential for living authentically and fostering self-love.
- Recognizing and nurturing your strengths and talents is fundamental to building self-esteem and discovering joy and purpose in life.
- Embracing your quirks and allowing yourself to dream big are vital steps in the journey of self-discovery, leading to a more fulfilling and authentic life.

CHAPTER 2
CULTIVATING POSITIVE SELF-TALK

One of the most powerful tools you can have in your toolkit is self-talk. This continuous stream of thoughts can be your greatest friend or your most formidable foe, depending on its nature. Understanding self-talk is important because it shapes how you view yourself and the world around you. Self-talk influences your confidence, decisions, and, ultimately, the path your life takes.

Self-talk is the inner voice that narrates your day-to-day experiences. It comments on your performance, how you look and interact with others, and much more. This voice can be kind and encouraging, or it can be critical, demeaning, and negative. The nature of your self-talk plays a big role in your mental and emotional well-being.

For many teen girls, the inner critic can be particularly loud. It might tell you that you're not good enough, smart enough, or pretty enough. These messages can hurt your self-esteem and reduce your ability to see your true worth.

The good news is that self-talk is a habit, and like any habit, it can be changed. The first step in transforming self-talk is to listen to your thoughts. Pay attention to the times when your inner voice is more critical than supportive. What triggers these thoughts? Are they tied to specific events, people, or feelings of inadequacy?

Once you start noticing patterns in your self-talk, you can question its credibility. Often, you'll find that these harsh judgments are not based on facts but rather on fears, insecurities, or past experiences that no longer serve you. Recognizing this is pivotal because it allows you to challenge and change these thought patterns.

Transforming negative self-talk into positive affirmations is not an overnight process. It requires patience, practice, and persistence. Start by gently correcting your inner critic. For instance, if you catch yourself thinking, "I'm not smart enough to ace this test," counter that thought with, "I have studied hard, and I am prepared. I can do this." Over time, these positive affirmations will become your new habit, slowly silencing the critic and empowering your inner cheerleader.

The goal is not to always have a positive inner voice—that's unrealistic. The aim is to have a more supportive inner voice that encourages you to do your best and bounce back from challenges. By transforming your self-talk, you're not just changing how you talk to yourself; you're changing how you live your life, filling it with more love and positivity.

HOW TO CHALLENGE NEGATIVE THOUGHTS

Another empowering step you can take is to challenge negative thoughts when they appear in your mind. If left unchecked, these thoughts can prevent you from recognizing your true potential. It's like having an internal critic who's always ready to point out your flaws, real or imagined. But here's a secret: you have the power to challenge and change this narrative.

First, start to notice when negative thoughts take hold of you. These thoughts may seem like truths but are twisted versions of our fears and insecurities. Recognizing these thoughts for what they are—distortions—is the first step in challenging them.

Once you've identified a negative thought, pause and ask yourself, "Is this really true?" More often than not, you'll find that these thoughts are based on feelings rather than facts. For instance, failing at a task doesn't mean you're a failure; it simply means you're human, and there's room for growth. By questioning your negative thoughts, you start to reduce their power over you.

Another powerful tool for challenging negative thoughts is countering them with evidence from your own life. For every thought that says you can't, remind yourself of the times you did. For every thought that says you're not enough, remember the moments you felt proud of yourself or when others appreciated you. This isn't about creating a false sense of self but balancing the narrative to include your strengths and achievements.

It's also helpful to talk to someone you trust about these thoughts. Sometimes, just voicing these insecurities can lessen their hold on you. A friend, family member, or mentor can offer a different perspective, helping you see yourself more positively.

Lastly, practice compassion towards yourself. Challenging negative thoughts isn't about being harsh or critical; it's about gently guiding yourself toward a more loving and accepting viewpoint. Imagine what you would say to a friend in a similar situation and offer encouragement to yourself. This act of self-compassion is a powerful antidote to negative thoughts.

As you continue to challenge and change the way you talk to yourself, the voice of your internal critic will become less daunting. This process requires patience and practice, and people work on it even as they pass their teenage years.

THE POWER OF AFFIRMATIONS

Another transformative practice you can adopt in the pursuit of self-love is the art of positive affirmations. These powerful statements are not just words; they are declarations of your worth, your capabilities, and your dreams. They can transform your inner dialogue from doubt to empowerment.

Affirmations are based on the principle that our thoughts shape our reality. When you repeatedly affirm your strengths and values, you shift your mindset, focusing on your potential rather than your limitations. This shift doesn't happen overnight, but with consistency, affirmations can rewire your brain to naturally think more positively.

To start, choose affirmations that you can relate to. They

should be statements that spark a light within you, even if a part of you doubts their truth. These statements should be in the present tense, as if they are already true, to help your mind accept them as your current reality. Here are some powerful starting points:

I am worthy of love and respect.

My feelings are valid and I honor my emotional needs.

I have the strength to overcome challenges and grow from them.

Doing my best is enough.

My potential is limitless and I can achieve my dreams.

I embrace my uniqueness and celebrate my individuality.

I am a powerful force of kindness and positivity in the world.

Incorporating affirmations into your day can be simple. You might repeat them in the mirror each morning, write them in your journal, or set reminders on your phone to affirm your worth throughout the day. The key is to engage with these affirmations regularly and with intention.

Affirmations help you approach the challenges you face in life with a mindset that empowers you to believe in yourself. They empower to navigate through them with positivity and confidence. Affirmations remind you of your inner strength and the incredible potential within you.

As you continue practicing affirmations, you'll notice a shift in how you view yourself and the world around you. This shift towards a positive mindset is crucial in your self-love journey.

HOW TO CREATE A POSITIVE MINDSET

What follows from positive affirmations is cultivating a positive mindset. This is not about ignoring the complexities and challenges of life but about choosing to focus on the light, even in darkness. It's about having an attitude that uplifts and supports you, especially when you encounter turbulence and self-doubt.

Creating a positive mindset begins with understanding that your thoughts have power. They can shape your reality, influence your emotions, and even affect your actions. Therefore, it's crucial to become mindful of the narrative that plays in your mind. Are your thoughts serving you, or are they your own harshest critic? The goal here is not to achieve perfection but to lean towards kindness and encouragement within your internal dialogue.

You could use some of the tools from earlier in this chapter to help you do this. For example, one effective way to shift towards a more positive mindset is to challenge negative thoughts when they arise. This doesn't mean you have to fight with every negative thought or judge yourself for having them. Instead, acknowledge them and gently guide your mind towards a more positive or realistic perspective. For instance, if you think, "I can't do anything right," pause and ask yourself, "Is this true?" Challenge this thought with evidence of your successes, no matter how small they may seem.

Another way to foster a positive mindset is to surround yourself with positivity. This includes the people you spend time with, the content you consume on social media, and even the environment you create for yourself. Seek out friendships and communities that uplift you and make you feel good about yourself. Fill your social media feed with accounts that inspire and motivate you rather than those that make you feel inadequate. Create a personal space where you can feel safe and happy.

There will be days when doing this feels effortless and others when it feels like an uphill battle. On those challenging days, remind yourself of your worth and the progress you've made.

As you continue to develop a positive mindset, you'll find that it enhances your relationship with yourself and the world around you. It becomes easier to find joy in the little things, bounce back from setbacks, and pursue your dreams. The light that shines from within you can illuminate the darkest of paths and guide you towards a life filled with self-love and happiness.

THE POWER OF GRATITUDE

Gratitude is a simple yet profound way to shift your focus from what's missing to the abundance of good things around you. Gratitude means valuing the little things in life, finding beauty in what you have, and seeing the value in challenges that make us stronger.

To start practicing gratitude, consider keeping a gratitude journal. Before you sleep, write down three things you're grateful for each night. These don't have to be big events; they can be as simple as a warm cup of tea on a cold morning, a compliment from a friend, or the comfort of your bed at the end of a long day. The act of writing them down shifts your focus and helps you see the positive aspects of your life more clearly.

Another way you can do this is to express gratitude towards others. This can be through a thank you note, a kind message, or a small act of kindness. Expressing gratitude not only brightens someone else's day but also reinforces your own feelings of thankfulness. It can also strengthen your relationships with others.

Gratitude can also be practiced through mindfulness and meditation. Taking a few moments each day to silently acknowledge what you're thankful for can create a sense of peace and contentment.

Here are some examples of things you could be grateful for today:

I am grateful for my friends who always know how to make me smile.

I am thankful for my family who always has my back and gives me advice, even when I don't want to hear it.

I am grateful for the chance to go to school and learn new things.

I am grateful for my body, which allows me to live my life each day.

I am thankful for my hobbies because let me express myself and unwind.

I am thankful for every mistake I've made because each one has taught me something important and made me stronger.

I am grateful for technology and all the resources I have access to because they connect me to a world of possibilities.

Practicing gratitude doesn't mean ignoring the difficulties in life. It's about finding a balance and acknowledging and appreciating the good alongside the bad. Gratitude can help you have a more positive outlook on life, improve your mental health, and increase your resilience.

By incorporating gratitude into your daily routine, you're taking a significant step towards enabling positive self-talk and having a more loving relationship with yourself. Gratitude is a gentle reminder that, in every moment, there is something to be thankful for. It's within this space of thankfulness that self-love flourishes.

CASE STUDY: LILY'S TRANSFORMATION THROUGH POSITIVE SELF-TALK AND GRATITUDE

As a 17-year-old high school senior, Lily constantly battled her inner critic. Despite her achievements, she struggled with feelings of inadequacy and self-doubt, often comparing herself unfavorably to her peers. This negative self-talk affected her confidence, relationships, and overall outlook on life.

One day, after a particularly disheartening encounter with her inner critic, Lily confided in her school counselor, Maya, who was known for her positive outlook on life. Maya listened with empathy before sharing her own journey of overcoming negative self-talk through the practices of positive affirmations and gratitude.

Inspired by her conversation with Maya, Lily embarked on her journey towards positive self-talk. She became more aware of her inner dialogue, especially when stressed or disappointed. Lily noticed that her inner critic was loudest when she faced challenges or made mistakes, often telling her she wasn't good enough or that she would never succeed.

Determined to change this mindset, Lily started challenging her negative thoughts. Whenever she caught herself being self-critical, she would pause and ask, "Why am I telling myself this?" She then countered these thoughts with proof of her capabilities and past successes, reminding herself what she was good at.

Lily also embraced the power of positive affirmations. Although they sounded silly to her at first, she would stand in front of her mirror each morning and affirm her worth, abilities, and potential. Phrases like "I am capable of achieving my goals," "I am worthy of love," and "I believe in myself" became her daily mantras. These affirmations slowly began to shift her mindset, replacing self-doubt with self-confidence.

Lily started keeping a gratitude journal to complement her positive self-talk practice. Every night before bed, she would write down something she was grateful for that day. Doing this helped Lily focus on the positive aspects of her life, from the support of her friends and family to the more minor things she appreciated in life. Expressing gratitude allowed her to see her struggles as chances to grow rather than as evidence of failure.

Lily's transformation didn't happen overnight, but with patience and persistence, she noticed a significant shift in her outlook on life. Her inner critic became less dominant, replaced by a supportive inner voice encouraging her to pursue her dreams and embrace her imperfections.

Through positive self-talk and gratitude, Lily learned to appreciate herself more and recognize her worth and potential. She discovered that changing how she talked to herself could change how she viewed her life, filling it with more love, joy, and fulfillment.

Lily's story shows the power of positive self-talk and gratitude and how it can transform your relationship with yourself.

CHAPTER SUMMARY

- Self-talk is the internal dialogue that influences your perception, confidence, and life decisions. Self-talk can be either positive or negative.
- Negative self-talk can impact your self-esteem and self-worth, but it's a habit that can be changed.
- Transforming self-talk involves becoming aware of and challenging your negative thoughts and replacing them with positive affirmations.
- Positive affirmations are powerful tools for shifting your mindset towards self-love and empowerment.
- Challenging negative thoughts requires recognizing their distortions, questioning their validity, and countering them with thoughts of your achievements.
- Creating a positive mindset involves mindfulness of your thoughts, challenging negativity, surrounding yourself with positivity, and practicing self-compassion.
- Practicing gratitude, such as keeping a gratitude journal or expressing thankfulness to others, shifts your focus from lack to abundance. Gratitude can enhance your mental health and resilience.
- Cultivating a positive mindset and self-talk, challenging negative thoughts, embracing affirmations, and practicing gratitude are all steps you can take toward embracing self-love.

CHAPTER 3
BUILDING HEALTHY RELATIONSHIPS

Healthy relationships can bring us joy, support, and help us grow. They are like mirrors, showing you not only how others see you but also your true self. Understanding this is especially crucial during your teenage years, a time full of big changes and challenges.

Relationships are all about the connection between individuals. This connection can be created through shared experiences, mutual respect, and understanding. It's about finding those who celebrate you and stand by you when times are tough. These relationships can help us feel like we belong and have a purpose.

However, not all relationships may serve our best interests. Some might stop us from growing or lead us away from the path of self-love. Being able to tell the difference is vital. It's important to learn how to spot relationships that are harmful or exhausting. This means paying attention to your gut feelings and noticing how you feel after spending time with different people. Do they uplift you, or leave you feeling tired and down? Answering these questions can help you choose who to let into your inner circle.

Healthy relationships are reciprocal. They are built on give-and-take, where both people contribute to each other's well-being. This ensures that the relationship is balanced and everyone feels valued and heard. It's about supporting each other's dreams and aspirations while also respecting each other's individuality.

Communication is key in helping these relationships grow. It's through open and honest communication that misunderstandings are cleared, and bonds are strengthened. Learning to express your thoughts and feelings respectfully and listen to others with an open heart will serve you well, not just in personal relationships but in all areas of life.

Remember that the relationships you invest in can impact your life in many ways. They can be a source of comfort, inspiration, and empowerment, helping you become the best version of yourself. So choose wisely and don't be afraid to make new connections.

UNDERSTANDING BOUNDARIES AND RESPECT

Understanding and establishing boundaries is a cornerstone of building healthy relationships. Boundaries are not walls meant to keep people out but rather guidelines that help us communicate our needs, respect ourselves, and gain respect from others. They are essential in all relationships, whether with friends, family, or romantic partners.

Imagine boundaries as invisible lines that help everyone understand what is acceptable and what is not. It's about knowing and expressing your limits comfortably and confidently. For example, if you feel overwhelmed by too much social interaction, it's okay to say, "I need some quiet time to recharge." This simple act of setting a boundary honors your need for space and teaches others how to treat you with the respect you deserve.

Respect, much like boundaries, is a two-way street. It involves listening to and honoring the boundaries of others just as much as asserting your own. When someone shares their boundaries with you, it shows they trust you. Respecting these limits strengthens the bond between you and the other person, creating mutual respect and understanding.

Setting boundaries and ensuring others respect them can be challenging. Know that saying no does not make you selfish or unkind. It means you are practicing self-respect and self-care, which are essential aspects of self-love.

It's also important to recognize that boundaries can change. Your needs might shift as you grow and evolve, and that's perfectly normal. Checking in with yourself and reassessing your boundaries is a healthy practice. Communicate these changes clearly and kindly to those around you, allowing your relationships to grow and adapt with you. We'll return to boundaries and how to set healthy ones in a later chapter.

Boundaries are especially important in friendships, which we will explore in the next section. Friendships are a vital part of our social lives and personal development. They can bring us support, joy, and companionship, but also need care and attention to flourish. By practicing setting and respecting boundaries, you lay the groundwork for meaningful and lasting connections with your friends.

HOW TO NAVIGATE FRIENDSHIPS

Navigating friendships during your teenage years can feel like sailing through uncharted waters. There are moments of smooth sailing, unexpected storms, and discoveries of beautiful islands that make the journey worthwhile. This section will help you steer through these waters with grace and confidence.

Friendships are one of life's greatest treasures. They can make us feel happy and supported and positively impact our well-being. However, not all friendships are created equal, and as you grow, your friendships will evolve, too. It's important to recognize that change, including your relationships with friends, is a natural part of life.

Making friends requires patience, care, and finding the right environment. It's about discovering shared interests or experiences, which can help friendships bloom. Be yourself because authenticity attracts genuine connections. Join clubs, sports, or groups that align with your interests, creating opportunities for friendships to form. Remember, a smile, kind words, or even something simple as saying hello can lead to a budding friendship. And just like in life, not every attempt will lead to a friendship, but with time and care, beautiful friendships can flourish, adding vibrant colors to your life.

Understand that it's okay to outgrow friendships. People change, and sometimes, the things you have in common with someone no longer align with who you are or want to be. This doesn't mean you have to completely cut ties or have a dramatic breakup. It simply means permitting yourself to move on, making room for new connections that better match your current self.

Make friends with people who make you feel good about yourself. True friends uplift you and support your dreams. They are the ones who celebrate your successes without jealousy and stand by you when times get tough. These friendships are built on respect, trust, and love for each other. When you find these special friends, make an effort to see them and stay connected. You'll never know; you may still be friends 20 years later!

Friendship is about quality, not quantity. Having a few close friends who truly understand and care for you is more valuable than having a large group of acquaintances.

Friendships are not restricted by age, gender, or location. You might find it easiest to become friends with people in your class or who are the same age as you. But be open to making friends with people from other walks of life. You may meet them through extracurricular activities, shared hobbies, or mutual friends.

As we explored earlier, communication is vital in maintaining healthy friendships. Be open and honest about your feelings, and be a good listener. Friendships thrive when you share and care about each other equally. If you find yourself constantly being the one giving and never receiving, it might be time to reassess that friendship.

Lastly, be yourself. The best friendships are those where you can be your true self, quirks and all, without fear of being judged or teased. These are the friendships that will stand the test of time.

Navigating friendships isn't easy in your teens. It's easy to get swept up by the crowd and want to be friends with the most popular, prettiest, or trendiest people in your school. But it may not be worth your time if these people aren't good friends and don't bring out the best in you.

Friendship requires following your gut, expressing your feelings, and respecting yourself. By understanding your worth and finding the people who recognize and celebrate it, you'll build a network of friendships that will support and enrich your life beyond your teenage years.

Every friendship teaches you something valuable about love, life, and the person you are becoming. Embrace these lessons with an open heart, and you'll find that navigating friendships isn't just about avoiding the storms but also about enjoying the voyage and the companions you meet along the way.

HOW TO DEAL WITH CONFLICT

Conflict will inevitably occur in your relationships. It's a natural part of human interaction, and dealing with these moments can strengthen or weaken our connections with others. As you navigate the ups and downs of teenage life, knowing how to deal with conflict is essential. This section will guide you through these challenging waters to help you emerge stronger and more self-aware.

Conflict, while uncomfortable, is not always bad. It's an opportunity for growth and deeper connection. When a disagreement arises, it's a sign that something needs attention. It could be a boundary being crossed, a need not being met, or a misunderstanding that needs to be clarified. By framing conflict this way, you can approach it with curiosity rather than fear.

Communication is the key to resolving conflict. However, effective communication is more than just talking; it's about listening, understanding, and expressing yourself with clarity and compassion. Start by listening to the other person's perspective without interrupting. This doesn't mean you agree with them, but it shows respect for their feelings and thoughts. When it's your turn to speak, use "I" statements to express your feelings and needs. For example, instead of saying, "You never listen to me," try, "I feel hurt when I don't feel heard." This approach makes you sound less defensive and opens the door to a more productive conversation.

Learn how to recognize and manage your emotions during a conflict. Emotions can run high, and it's easy to react impulsively when you're hurt or angry. However, taking a moment to breathe and calm yourself can significantly affect the outcome. Taking a break from the conversation is okay if you feel overwhelmed. Sometimes, a little space can provide the clarity you need to approach the situation constructively.

Conflict resolution is a skill that requires practice and patience. Not every disagreement will have the outcome you want, and that's okay. What matters is your commitment to treating yourself and others with respect and compassion, even in challenging moments. By embracing conflict as an opportunity for growth, you're building stronger relationships and a deeper sense of self-love.

Your relationship with yourself sets the tone for every other relationship in your life. Embracing self-love in relationships means honoring your feelings, setting healthy boundaries, and treating yourself with the same compassion and respect you offer to others. Self-love empowers you to navigate the complexities of relationships confidently, ensuring that you build truly enriching and supportive connections. Let's explore this more in the next section.

SELF-LOVE IN RELATIONSHIPS

As we navigate through the complexities of teenage years, the relationships we form play an important role in shaping our self-perception and how we engage with the world around us. Self-love guides you, keeps you grounded, and ensures you don't lose yourself when connecting with others.

Self-love in relationships is about recognizing your worth and value independently of anyone else's validation or approval. It's about setting boundaries that protect your emotional well-being and making choices that respect and care for yourself. When you love yourself, you are empowered to form more healthy, supportive, and enriching relationships.

One of the most beautiful aspects of self-love is how it transforms how you relate to others. It encourages you to seek connections that uplift and inspire you rather than those that drain you. It teaches you to be compassionate towards yourself and others, leading to more healthy and fulfilling relationships.

Embracing self-love in relationships also means being brave enough to walk away from situations that harm you. It's about knowing that you deserve to be treated well and refusing to settle for anything less. This might require difficult conversations and tough decisions, but it's crucial to honoring your worth.

Remember, every experience, whether positive or negative, offers valuable lessons that help you grow and better understand what it means to love and be loved healthily.

Self-love is the key to building and sustaining healthy relationships. It's the shield that protects us, the guide that leads us, and the light that illuminates our path to deeper, more meaningful connections. Remember that the most important relationship you will ever have is with yourself.

CASE STUDY: EMMA'S JOURNEY TO SELF-RESPECT AND HEALTHY FRIENDSHIPS

Emma, a 14-year-old high school student, struggled with the dynamics of her main friendship group. Initially, she felt lucky to be included in what many considered the "popular" group. However, as time passed, Emma felt uncomfortable with how the group treated others and herself. They often made plans without consulting her, dismissed her opinions, and sometimes made fun of her interests in art and literature, labeling them as "boring" or "nerdy."

Emma's discomfort reached a tipping point when her friends pressured her to skip a much-anticipated art workshop to attend a party. She realized that she was sacrificing her interests and values to fit in with a group that didn't respect her boundaries or appreciate her for who she was.

Feeling isolated and conflicted, Emma turned to her older sister, Ava, for advice. Ava listened without judgment and encouraged Emma to reflect on what truly made her happy and to think about whether her current friendships aligned with those values.

Emma decided to make a change. She started by setting a boundary with her friends, choosing to attend the art workshop instead of the party. As expected, her decision was met with ridicule, confirming her feelings that these friendships were not healthy for her.

In the following weeks, Emma began exploring new activities that aligned more closely with her interests. She joined the school's art club and volunteered at a local community center, where she met other teenagers who shared her passion for creativity and literature. Gradually, Emma formed new friendships built on respect, shared interests, and support.

Through this transition, Emma learned the value of respecting herself and surrounding herself with people who inspired and appreciated her. She discovered true friends celebrate your successes without jealousy and respect your decisions.

Reflecting on her experience, Emma realized that true friendships aren't just about avoiding negative influences but also about embracing the journey of self-discovery and the joy of connecting with like-minded people. Emma's journey wasn't easy, but it taught her that self-love and setting boundaries are crucial for building healthy, fulfilling relationships. Emma's story shows the power of self-respect and the beauty of finding friendships that enrich your life.

CHAPTER SUMMARY

- Relationships are crucial for joy, support, and growth, acting as mirrors for self-reflection, especially during your teenage years.
- Meaningful relationships are based on shared experiences, mutual respect, and understanding. They can help you feel a sense of belonging and purpose.
- Identifying and avoiding toxic relationships hindering your personal growth is important. Instead, focus on relationships that uplift you and support self-love.

- Healthy relationships are built on give-and-take, ensuring everyone feels valued and heard, supporting each other's dreams, and respecting individuality.
- Communication is key in healthy relationships, with open and honest dialogue clearing misunderstandings and strengthening bonds.
- Establishing and respecting boundaries is essential in all relationships, serving as guidelines for communicating needs and fostering respect for each other.
- Navigating friendships involves being open and honest and seeking out those who inspire and support you.
- Self-love in relationships means recognizing your own worth, setting boundaries for emotional well-being, and pursuing healthy, supportive connections.

CHAPTER 4
EMBRACING YOUR BODY

Imagine walking in a garden full of different, beautiful flowers. Each one is special in its own way, but all are equally stunning. Your body is like one of these beautiful flowers in the big garden of people.

Body image is your view of yourself when you look in the

mirror or think about your appearance. It includes what you think about your looks, your feelings about your body's size, shape, and weight, and how you feel and control your body when you move. It's a mix of thoughts, feelings, and perceptions that can change like the ocean's tides.

Self-esteem is how much you value yourself. It is closely connected to self-respect and self-worth. Imagine self-esteem as the soil that nourishes the roots of your personal garden. When the soil is rich and well cared for, the plants that grow are strong and vibrant. In the same way, strong self-esteem helps you maintain a positive view of your body.

Keeping a positive view of your body and self-esteem can be tricky, especially in today's society, where media and social expectations often dictate beauty standards. Comparing yourself to unrealistic ideals and striving for perfection can turn into a struggle with your body image, harming your confidence and self-love.

But here's the empowering truth: your body is incredible in so many ways. It's what carries you through life's adventures. Every scar, every curve, every freckle reflects your uniqueness. Learning to appreciate your body for its strength and capability rather than just its appearance is crucial to fostering a healthy body image and self-esteem.

Overcoming body image issues is a step in your journey toward self-love and acceptance. Start by practicing compassion towards yourself. Surround yourself with positive influences—friends and media that celebrate all body types and encourage self-care over perfection. Remember, your appearance doesn't measure your worth. Focus on what your body can do, not just how it looks. Practice gratitude for your body's capabilities, whether dancing to your favorite song, laughing until your stomach hurts, or simply taking a deep breath. Challenge negative thoughts with gentleness and remind yourself that beauty is diverse and unique, just like you. It's okay to have tough days, but remember, you're more than a reflection in the mirror—you're a wonderful blend of talents, dreams, and experiences.

Self-esteem grows when you challenge and overcome negative thoughts about your body. It's a journey of small steps, of choosing to see the beauty in difference and the strength in individuality.

Just like a garden thrives with a variety of flowers, the world is enriched by the diversity of its people. Embracing and celebrating this diversity is not just an act of self-love but a reminder that beauty comes in all forms.

CELEBRATING DIVERSITY

Each of us is a unique masterpiece, intricately designed with differences that make us who we are. Recognizing and honoring the variety of body shapes, sizes, colors, and abilities in the world around us is essential. This celebration is about acknowledging these differences and learning to see them as a source of strength and beauty.

There is no single standard for beauty. Society often presents a very narrow view of what it means to be attractive, but this perspective doesn't reflect the rich diversity of human life. Your individuality is what makes you uniquely beautiful. By embracing this truth, you can begin to free yourself from comparisons and embrace your beauty with confidence.

Celebrating diversity also means appreciating your body for what it is capable of rather than focusing only on how it looks. Your body allows you to experience the world, express emotions, and engage in activities you love. Recognizing and valuing these abilities can shift your perspective from criticism to gratitude.

Be kind and compassionate towards others and their bodies. Choosing to spread positivity and acceptance can make a big difference in a world where judgment and body shaming are all too common. It's about creating a supportive community where everyone feels valued and respected, regardless of appearance.

BUILDING HEALTHY HABITS

Healthy habits are not just about what you eat or how often you exercise. They help you build a relationship with your body that is kind, forgiving, and supportive. Let's explore how you can form healthy habits in a way that feels empowering and sustainable.

Start by listening to your body's cues and responding with care. This means eating when you're hungry, resting when you're tired, and moving in ways that bring you joy. It's not about strict diets or rigorous exercise routines; it's about balance and finding what makes your body feel good.

Incorporate a variety of foods into your diet that nourish your body and soul. There's no need to label foods as "good" or "bad." Instead, aim for a colorful plate filled with fruits, vegetables, proteins, and grains you enjoy. Listen to your body's needs and cravings, and fulfill them with a balance of nutrients and treats. Your relationship with food should be one of enjoyment and nourishment, not punishment or guilt. Remember, it's perfectly okay to indulge in your favorite treats. The key is moderation, not deprivation.

Physical activity is also an excellent way to care for your body. Exercise not only improves physical health but also boosts mental well-being. Find a form of movement you genuinely enjoy, whether dancing, yoga, walking with your friends, or playing a team sport. The goal is to move your body in ways that feel joyful and stimulating, not tedious or overwhelming.

Sleep is another crucial healthy habit. Your body needs time to rest and recharge, so aim for 7-9 hours of sleep each night. Create a calming bedtime routine that signals to your body it's time to wind down. This might include reading, gentle stretching, or listening to soothing music. Listen to your body when it signals that it's tired or overwhelmed, and respond with kindness by giving it the rest it deserves.

Lastly, hydration is vital. Drinking enough water each day helps your body function at its best. Carry a water bottle with you as a reminder to drink regularly. If you find water too bland, try adding fruit slices or a splash of juice for a hint of flavor.

Adopting healthy habits is a form of self-love and self-care. It's about making choices that honor your body's needs and improve your well-being. Be patient with yourself as you explore what habits work best for you. It's a process of trial and error, and it's okay to adjust your approach as you learn more about what makes you feel your best.

HOW TO DEAL WITH BODY SHAMING

One of the hurdles you might face during your teenage years is body shaming. It's an unfortunate reality that, at some point, you may encounter negative comments or attitudes about your body from others. These can come from peers, social media, and sometimes, even from family members. It's vital to understand that body shaming is more about the other person's unresolved issues and not a reflection of your worth or beauty.

First and foremost, know that your worth isn't lessened

because someone else might not recognize your value. You are so much more than a body. You are a lively soul with dreams, passions, and the ability to change the world. Your body carries you through this life, and it should be treated with care and love, not negativity.

When faced with body shaming, return to your positive thinking and self-love practices. This means actively appreciating your body for what it can do rather than how it looks. Celebrate the small things, like how your legs carry you through your day or how your arms allow you to hug your loved ones. These may seem simple, but they are profound acts of gratitude towards yourself.

Surround yourself with friends and family who uplift and remind you of your worth. Surround yourself with positivity and limit your exposure to toxic environments or social media accounts that make you feel inadequate. Remember, you can curate your social media feed with accounts that celebrate body diversity and promote self-love.

Be kind to yourself. When negative thoughts about your body arise, challenge them with positive affirmations. Remind yourself that perfection is an unattainable and unnecessary goal. You are perfectly imperfect, and that's what makes you special.

If body shaming is affecting your mental health, don't be afraid to seek support from a trusted adult, counselor, or therapist. Sometimes, having someone else guide you through these feelings can provide the tools you need to navigate them more effectively. You are worthy of love and respect, just as you are. Embrace your body because it is the only one you have and is beautiful.

CASE STUDY: MIA'S PATH TO BODY POSITIVITY AND SELF-LOVE

Mia, a 15-year-old high school sophomore, always felt out of place in her skin. Growing up, she was taller and more muscular than most of her peers, which made her feel self-conscious and, at times, less feminine. Mia's discomfort with her body was compounded by the endless stream of perfect images she saw on social media and the occasional thoughtless comments from classmates and even family members.

One day, during a physical education class, Mia overheard a group of students making fun of her athletic build. The comments hurt her, and she spent the rest of the day trying to shrink herself and appear smaller and less noticeable. That night, Mia shared her feelings with her best friend, Lena.

Lena listened intently before sharing her own journey of coming to love her body. She emphasized the importance of self-compassion and the realization that bodies are meant to be diverse and capable, not just things to look at. Lena introduced Mia to body positivity and showed Mia some inspirational figures she followed on social media who advocate for self-love and body diversity.

Inspired by her conversation with Lena, Mia began to curate her social media feeds, unfollowing accounts that made her feel inadequate and seeking out those that celebrated all body types. She discovered a community of people who celebrated their unique features and spoke openly about the journey to self-acceptance. This was a revelation for Mia, who had never considered that her athletic build could be a source of strength and beauty.

Mia also started to explore activities that made her appreciate her body for what it could do rather than how it looked. She joined the school's track team, where her height and strength became her greatest assets. Running gave Mia a sense of freedom and confidence. She loved the feeling of her muscles powering her forward. She began to see her body as a capable and incredible vessel for her passions.

As Mia's perspective shifted, she found herself more willing to stand up against body shaming, not just directed at her but also at others. She became an advocate for body positivity among her peers, encouraging them to see their own beauty and strength. Mia's journey wasn't without its challenges, but with each step, she grew more confident in her skin.

Mia's transformation also had a ripple effect on her friends and family. Her newfound self-assurance and advocacy for body diversity inspired those around her to reconsider their own views on beauty and self-worth.

Mia learned that self-esteem blooms from within, nurtured by self-respect, kindness, and the celebration of one's capabilities. She discovered that beauty is not a one-size-fits-all concept but a diverse garden where every flower thrives by simply being its unique self. Mia's path to body positivity and self-love was a journey back to herself, recognizing and embracing the beauty of her natural self. Mia's story is a testament to the power of self-love and the importance of celebrating the unique beauty in everyone.

CHAPTER SUMMARY

- Understanding the relationship between body image and self-esteem is essential for embracing your body.

- Body image involves perceptions, feelings, and thoughts about your appearance, which can change over time and be influenced by societal standards.
- Self-esteem is the overall value you place on yourself and can help you maintain a positive body image.
- Today's media and societal beauty standards can make it hard to maintain a positive body image and self-esteem, leading to comparisons and unrealistic expectations.
- Embracing your body and appreciating it for its capabilities is vital to fostering a healthy body image and self-esteem.
- Practicing kindness towards yourself, celebrating your body's abilities, and challenging negative thoughts can help improve self-esteem and body image.
- Celebrating diversity and recognizing the beauty in different body shapes, sizes, and abilities enriches your self-acceptance and contributes to a more inclusive world.
- Developing healthy habits, dealing with body shaming through self-love and support, and practicing self-care are essential for fostering a positive relationship with your body.

CHAPTER 5
FINDING YOUR CREATIVE SIDE

Finding and growing your creative side is a vital part of loving yourself and growing as a person. Being creative isn't just about making art or writing stories; it's about expressing yourself in your unique way. It's about enjoying creating something, no matter the result.

Everyone has a unique creative spark waiting to be ignited. It might be in how you see the world, the ideas that dance through your mind, or the hobbies that make your heart sing. The key is to allow yourself to explore and experiment without judgment or fear of failure. Creativity is not a competition. It's a personal journey of exploration and expression.

To find your creative spark, start by paying attention to the activities that make you lose track of time, the topics that light up your eyes when you talk about them, and the dreams that fill you with excitement. These are clues pointing towards your passions and interests. Allow yourself to follow these clues with curiosity and openness. Try new things, even if they seem daunting at first. You might discover a love for something you never expected.

Another powerful way to ignite your creativity is to create a creativity journal. This journal can be a space where you jot down ideas, sketch, write poems, or insert pictures that inspire you. There's no right or wrong way to use it; the goal is simply to make space for your thoughts and inspirations. Over time, this journal can become a treasure trove of ideas and a reminder of your creative journey.

If you don't know where to start, here are some activities you can try to channel your creative energy:

- Writing poetry or short stories
- Drawing in a sketchbook
- Coloring in or painting
- Creating digital art or graphic design
- Starting a DIY fashion or jewelry project
- Experimenting with photography or videography
- Designing and creating a personal blog or vlog
- Learning to play a musical instrument or write songs

- Exploring different types of dance or choreography
- Crafting handmade gifts or decorations for your room

Don't be afraid to share your creations with others. Sharing can be scary, but it can also be incredibly rewarding. It's a way to connect with others, receive feedback, and grow as a creator. Remember that everyone was once a beginner. What matters most is that you're taking steps to express yourself and bring your unique perspective to the world.

Embracing your creativity will enrich your life and inspire those around you. Your creative spark is a gift; the world is waiting to see what you'll do with it. So explore, create, and let your light shine brightly.

HOW TO OVERCOME CREATIVE BLOCKS

Encountering creative blocks is a natural part of the creative process. While frustrating, these blocks are not barriers but stepping stones toward deeper self-understanding and growth. Embracing your creative blocks with consideration and curiosity can transform them from obstacles to opportunities.

Creative blocks often signal a need for rest or a change of perspective. Your mind is a garden that requires both sunshine and rain; periods of intense creativity must be balanced with rest and replenishment. When you hit a block, it might be your inner self telling you it's time to take a break. Break up your creative time with activities that make you feel happy and relaxed, whether reading, walking outside, or spending time with loved ones. These moments of rest are not a detour from your creative path but an essential part of the process.

Comparison can be the thief of joy and creativity. In a world amplified by social media, it's easy to fall into the trap of comparing yourself to others. Remember, your creativity is as unique as your fingerprint and cannot be compared to anyone else's. When you are caught in the comparison spiral, gently guide your focus back to your own path. Celebrate your creativity and progress, no matter how small it may seem.

You could embrace the power of journaling to unlock your creative blocks. Writing down your thoughts, fears, and dreams can clarify your emotions and ideas, allowing new inspiration. Sometimes, the act of writing can reveal hidden insights and solutions that were buried within you. Allow your journal to be a safe space where your creativity can flow, free from judgment.

Lastly, seek inspiration in the world around you. This could mean spending time in nature, visiting art galleries, reading books, or listening to music that moves you. Explore new hobbies, engage with different art forms, and open yourself to new experiences. Inspiration can be found everywhere, but you must be open to receiving it. Sometimes, the simplest experiences can spark the most profound ideas.

Overcoming creative blocks is not about forcing inspiration but nourishing your creativity with patience and love. Each block invites you to explore deeper aspects of yourself and your passion. By approaching these challenges with openness and positivity, you'll discover that the path beyond the block is richer and more rewarding than you imagined.

HOW TO SET GOALS FOR YOUR PROJECTS

After overcoming creative blocks, it's time to take a step forward by setting goals for your passion projects. This process is not just about achieving outcomes but also about understanding yourself better and appreciating your unique talents.

Setting goals begins with clarity. Ask yourself, "What do I love doing so much that time seems to fly by when I'm doing it?" Whether writing, painting, coding, or anything else that sets your heart on fire, identifying this passion is the first step. Once you know your passions, it's time to dream big. Allow yourself to envision the most magnificent possibilities from your passion. Remember, this is your personal canvas, and you're free to paint it with the colors of your wildest dreams.

Dreams and passions need a structure to thrive, which is where goal setting comes into play. Start by breaking down your big dream into smaller, achievable goals. These should be specific, measurable, attainable, relevant, and time-bound (SMART).

For example, if your dream is to become a writer, a SMART goal could be to write at least 500 words daily or to finish the first draft of a short story within three months. By setting such goals, you're creating a roadmap that will guide you toward your larger vision.

Be flexible with your goal-setting process. Sometimes, the path to our dreams takes unexpected turns, and that's okay. Being open to change and adapting your goals shows strength and self-awareness. Each step you take and goal you achieve brings you closer to finding your passions and, ultimately, yourself.

As you explore your creativity and passions, remember to celebrate every milestone, no matter how small it may seem. Celebrating your achievements is an act of self-love that reinforces your belief in your abilities and boosts your motivation to keep moving forward. Whether it's finishing a sketch, learning a new chord on the guitar, or writing a poem that speaks your truth, every achievement shows your dedication and love for your passion.

Your passion and creativity projects are not just tasks to be completed; they are expressions of your deepest self. They deserve to be pursued with love and enthusiasm and are just as crucial to your well-being as other aspects of your life. In the next section, you'll discover the importance of discipline in bringing your passion projects to life.

THE ROLE OF DISCIPLINE

Discipline is a word that often conjures images of strict schedules and rules, but in the realm of personal growth and self-love, discipline is something far more gentle and empowering.

Think of discipline not as a set of constraints but as a way to guide you toward your goals. It's about honoring your commitments to yourself, dreams, and passions. When you set goals for your passion projects, you take the first step in a dance with discipline. The following steps involve maintaining momentum, staying focused, and navigating the inevitable challenges that arise so you can achieve your goals.

Discipline means creating a physical and mental space where your creativity can flourish. It's about setting aside time regularly, even if it's just a few minutes each day, to dedicate to your passion projects. This consistent effort builds a structure of commitment and progress toward your goals.

It also involves setting boundaries. In a world filled with distractions, discipline helps you say no to things that might divert your attention and energy away from what truly matters to you. This is about making empowered choices that align with your passion and creativity.

Discipline also teaches you resilience. Not every attempt will be a success, and not every day will feel productive. However, the discipline of showing up for yourself and your passions, even on the tough days, builds an invaluable strength. In these moments, you learn the most about yourself and your passions. You discover new ways to overcome obstacles and find that your creativity isn't just about the highs but also about navigating the lows with positivity and determination.

Discipline in the context of self-love and creativity is not about perfection. It's about progress. It's about showing up and committing to yourself again and again. This disciplined approach isn't a straight path; it's a journey with twists and turns. Each step forward shows your love for yourself and dedication to your dreams.

As you continue to weave discipline into your life, you'll find that it becomes less about external factors and more about internal motivation. It becomes a part of your self-love language, a way to honor your creativity, passion, and, most importantly, yourself.

CELEBRATING YOUR ACHIEVEMENTS

Recognizing and celebrating your achievements is as crucial as the discipline and hard work that got you there. This celebration is not just a reward; it's a vital part of fostering your creativity and passion.

When you take the time to celebrate your achievements, you're sending a powerful message to yourself: that you are worthy of praise, your efforts matter, and you are capable of achieving great things. This can boost your self-esteem, increase your motivation, and fuel your desire to pursue your passions with even more vigor.

But how do you celebrate your achievements in a way that truly honors your journey and encourages your creative spirit? First, celebration doesn't always mean a grand gesture. Sometimes, the most meaningful celebrations are the quiet moments of reflection and gratitude for how far you've come.

One way to celebrate is by keeping a journal of your achievements. This can be a place where you record the milestones you've reached and express your feelings and thoughts about your journey. Writing down your achievements helps solidify them in your mind and allows you to look back and see your progress.

Another way to celebrate is by sharing your successes with others. This could mean telling a friend or family member about a goal you've reached or sharing your creative work with a broader audience. Sharing your achievements not only multiplies your joy but also inspires others to pursue their own passions and goals.

Celebrate in a way that feeds your soul and recharges your creative energy. This could be as simple as taking a day off to do something you love or treating yourself to something special. Do something that makes you feel joyful and alive, something that reminds you why you embarked on this journey in the first place.

Celebrating your achievements is not about ego or boasting. It's about honoring your hard work and creative spirit. It encourages you to keep pushing forward, exploring your passions, and embracing your unique path.

CHAPTER SUMMARY

- Discovering your creative spark can be an important part of self-love and personal growth. It is a form of self-expression and helps you find joy in creation.

- Creativity is a personal journey that requires allowing yourself to explore without fear of judgment or failure. It's not just limited to traditional arts.
- To ignite creativity, focus on activities that you find fun and engaging, and surround yourself with inspiration.
- Sharing your creations with others can be rewarding and is a step towards growth and connection. Remember that everyone once started as a beginner.
- Overcoming creative blocks involves recognizing the need for rest, avoiding comparison, journaling thoughts and fears, and seeking inspiration from the world.
- Setting goals for your passion projects requires clarity, dreaming big, and creating a structured plan with specific, achievable goals.
- Discipline is about self-respect, maintaining momentum, setting boundaries, and learning resilience through the ups and downs of the creative process.
- Celebrating your achievements and progress, no matter how small, boosts your self-esteem and motivation and is a vital part of the creative journey.

CHAPTER 6
MANAGING STRESS AND ANXIETY

Your teenage years are full of change, growth, and exploration. Stress and anxiety are a natural part of life, even during these years. It's not just about the big exams or the social dynamics; it's also about the internal questions and the process of figuring out who you are and where you fit in this vast world. This period of your life is marked by a quest for independence, together with puberty's physical and emotional changes. It can sometimes feel like riding a rollercoaster without a seatbelt.

Understanding that stress and anxiety are natural responses to the pressures and expectations faced during these years is the first step towards managing them. It's okay to feel overwhelmed by the demands of school, relationships, and future plans. It's okay to feel nervous about fitting in or standing out. These feelings are all part of the human experience, but they don't need to define you.

Stress is your body's reaction to change that requires an adjustment or response. Stress can appear in various ways, including physical symptoms like headaches or fatigue, emotional symptoms like irritability or sadness, and behavioral symptoms like withdrawing from activities or changes in eating habits.

Anxiety, on the other hand, is a feeling of fear, dread, or unease about what's to come. Anxiety might make you feel like you're in a constant state of worry or fear, even about things that might seem small to others. It's important to recognize these signs in yourself as signals that your body and mind are asking for attention and care.

One of the most empowering things you can do for yourself is to learn how to navigate these feelings. This doesn't mean pushing them away or pretending they don't exist. Instead, it's about acknowledging them, understanding their cause, and finding healthy ways to manage them. Whether it's through talking to someone you trust, writing down your thoughts, or doing things that bring you joy and relaxation, there are countless ways to support yourself through these feelings.

You are not alone in feeling stress or anxiety. These feelings don't have to be your enemies; they can be your teachers, guiding you toward a better understanding of yourself and your needs. By facing them with compassion, you're taking a significant step on your path to self-love and resilience.

MINDFULNESS AND RELAXATION TECHNIQUES

Mindfulness and relaxation techniques can help guide you through stressful or anxious moments. They can help you feel more at peace and discover your inner strength.

Practicing Mindfulness

Mindfulness is about being fully present in the moment and engaging with your experiences and feelings without judgment. It's like stepping back and observing your thoughts and feelings like leaves floating down a river. You notice and acknowledge them but don't have to pick them up.

You can start practicing mindfulness by dedicating a few minutes each day to simply breathe and be. Sit in a quiet space, close your eyes, and focus on your breath. Inhale deeply, feeling your chest and belly rise, and exhale slowly, feeling a sense of release. Whenever your mind wanders, gently bring your focus back to your breath. This simple act can be incredibly powerful and can help reduce feelings of anxiety.

Progressive Muscle Relaxation

Another powerful technique is progressive muscle relaxation. This involves tensing each muscle group in your body tightly, but not to the point of strain, and then slowly relaxing them. Start from your toes and work your way up to your head. With each tension and release, imagine the stress melting away from your body. This method not only helps with reducing anxiety but also promotes a deeper awareness of your physical self.

Visualization

Visualization is another tool you can add to your self-love toolkit. It involves picturing a place where you feel completely at ease. This could be a real place you've visited or a landscape you created in your mind. Focus on the details—the sounds, the smells, the colors. Feel the peace or happiness that this place brings you. This technique can be a powerful way to shift your focus away from stress and towards a sense of calm.

Journaling

Journaling is also a form of mindfulness that can help you understand and manage your emotions. It's a space where you can express yourself freely without fear of judgment. Write about what you're feeling, why you might be feeling this way, and anything else that comes to mind. Sometimes, the mere act of putting your thoughts on paper can provide relief and help clarify what you're feeling.

Incorporating these mindfulness and relaxation techniques into your daily routine can be transformative. They are not just practices for managing stress and anxiety but are also acts of self-care. By taking the time to nurture your mind and body, you're sending a powerful message to yourself—that you are worthy of care and attention.

THE IMPORTANCE OF SELF-CARE

One of the best things you can do to improve your mental well-being is to practice self-care. Self-care is not just about pampering yourself, though that can be a part of it. It's about caring for your body and listening to what it needs. It's about setting aside time to attend to your well-being, no matter how brief. This section will guide you through the various ways you can practice self-care.

Self-care is about looking after your mental, emotional, and physical well-being. It can be as simple as setting aside time for activities that make you feel happy and relaxed, such as reading a book, taking a long bath, or spending time in nature.

Self-care is also about listening to your body and mind. It's recognizing when you're pushing yourself too hard or on the brink of burnout, whether in physical activities, social engagements, or academic pressures. It's about understanding that saying 'no' to additional responsibilities isn't a sign of weakness but a profound act of self-respect.

Remember, you can't pour from an empty cup. By caring for yourself, you ensure you have the energy and health to pursue your dreams and support those you love.

Another aspect of self-care is hygiene. Taking care of your body by keeping it clean and groomed is a basic yet profound way of showing love for yourself. Whether it's a refreshing shower, a soothing bath, or a skincare routine, these acts of cleanliness can be incredibly grounding and signal to yourself that you are worth taking care of.

Incorporating self-care into your daily life doesn't have to be overwhelming. Start small. It could be as simple as ensuring you're hydrated, taking a few deep breaths to center yourself during a busy day, or setting aside time each week to engage in an activity that brings you joy. Here are some examples of self-care activities you could incorporate into your routine:

- Writing in a journal to express your thoughts and feelings
- Practicing yoga or meditation for relaxation and mindfulness
- Creating art, like drawing or painting, to channel creativity
- Taking a digital detox day to reduce screen time and recharge
- Listening to your favorite music or podcasts
- Engaging in physical activities, such as dancing, hiking, or playing a sport
- Going for a walk outside on a sunny day
- Spending time with pets can boost your mood and provide companionship
- Trying out new hobbies, like cooking or photography, to discover new passions
- Having a bubble bath at the end of a tiring day

Self-care is deeply personal, and what works for one person may not work for another. Try to explore different practices and find what makes you feel the most happy and connected to your body. This could range from simple daily routines to more elaborate self-care rituals. Stay in tune with yourself and be open to changing your self-care practices as your needs and circumstances change.

When you practice self-care, you're taking care of your body and mind and building a foundation of love and respect for yourself. Self-care is an essential part of managing stress and anxiety.

It's a practice that improves your relationship with yourself and equips you to face life's challenges with resilience. It's also about honoring your body for all it does for you, treating it with the care it deserves, and giving yourself some 'me' time. Self-care is not selfish; it's a necessary and beautiful part of loving and caring for yourself.

HOW TO SET HEALTHY BOUNDARIES

Setting healthy boundaries is another pivotal way to manage stress and anxiety. This practice is about saying no to what you don't want and affirming what you need for your mental, emotional, and physical well-being. It's about understanding and respecting your limits and ensuring others do too.

Imagine your energy as a beautiful garden. Just as a garden needs a fence to protect it from being trampled, you need boundaries to protect your energy. Without these boundaries, it's easy to overextend yourself, leading to stress and anxiety. But with them, you create a safe space for your garden to flourish.

Setting boundaries can start with tuning into your feelings. Notice situations that leave you feeling drained or uncomfortable. These feelings are signals, indicating where you need to set a limit. For example, if you are overwhelmed by too many extracurricular activities, it might be time to limit how many activities you do during the week.

Communicating your boundaries is equally important. It's okay to express your needs respectfully and clearly. You might worry about how others will react, but setting boundaries is fundamental to your well-being. Those who care for you will respect your limits and support you.

Enforcing your boundaries is also crucial. Sometimes, you

might need to remind others or distance yourself from those who consistently disrespect your limits. This isn't easy, but it's necessary for your mental health and self-love journey.

Here are some examples of the types of boundaries you could think about setting in your life.

Digital Communication Boundaries

Setting specific times when you aren't available for texting or social media to ensure you have time for homework, self-care, and rest. For example, "I don't check my phone after 9 PM so I can unwind and get a good night's sleep."

Personal Space Boundaries

Communicating your need for personal space, especially in crowded settings or at home. "I need my own space to relax and recharge. Please knock before entering my room."

Emotional Boundaries

Expressing when you are not in a place to take on someone else's emotional baggage or solve their problems. "I care about you, but I'm feeling overwhelmed myself and can't give you the support you need right now."

Academic Boundaries

Saying no to requests that interfere with your study time or academic goals. "I can't hang out on weeknights because I need to focus on my studies."

Physical Boundaries

Being clear about your comfort level with physical touch, even with friends or family. "I'm not really a hugger. I prefer a high-five or a wave."

Privacy Boundaries

Setting limits on sharing your personal information, both online and in person. "I'm not comfortable sharing that story about myself. Let's talk about something else."

Time Management Boundaries

Prioritizing your time and commitments, and saying no to additional responsibilities when necessary. "I appreciate the offer, but I have too much on my plate right now to commit to another project."

Your boundaries can change, and that's okay. As you grow and your life changes, your needs will too. Regularly reflect on your boundaries to ensure they still serve you well.

By setting and respecting healthy boundaries, you protect your well-being and teach others how to treat you. It empowers you to manage stress and anxiety more effectively, paving the way for a more balanced and fulfilling life.

SEEKING SUPPORT WHEN NEEDED

Seeking support is a brave step. It acknowledges that sometimes, the weight we carry is too heavy to bear alone. This doesn't mean you're not strong enough; it means you're wise enough to understand the power of community and connection.

Seeking support can take many forms, and finding what resonates with you is essential. Sometimes, it's about opening up to a trusted friend or family member. Sharing your feelings and experiences can provide a sense of relief and release. It's like letting someone else help you carry your backpack on a long hike. Remember, those who care about you want to support you, even if they might not always know how. Be open with them about what kind of support you need, whether it's a listening ear, advice, or just their presence.

Professional support is another powerful resource. Counselors, therapists, and mental health professionals are trained to help you navigate your feelings and find strategies to manage stress and anxiety. There's no shame in seeking their help; it's a sign of strength and a step towards healing. These professionals can offer you tools and insights that friends and family might not be able to provide, helping you build resilience and a deeper understanding of yourself.

Support groups can offer an incredibly comforting sense of community. Knowing you're not alone in your feelings and experiences can be validating and empowering. These groups provide a safe space to share and learn from others walking a similar path. They remind us that our struggles are part of the human experience, not a reflection of our capabilities.

Seeking support is an act of self-love. It acknowledges that you deserve to feel better and to live a life not dominated by stress and anxiety. It's a step towards embracing your vulnerability as a strength. By reaching out, you're helping yourself and paving the way for others to do the same. You're showing that it's okay not to be okay and that healing is possible with the right support.

As you navigate the waters of seeking support, be patient and kind to yourself. Finding the right type of help and people to support you can take time. But each step you take, no matter how small, is a step towards a more loving relationship with yourself.

CASE STUDY: ALEX'S JOURNEY THROUGH STRESS AND SELF-DISCOVERY

Alex, a 17-year-old high school junior, found themselves caught in a whirlwind of stress and anxiety. With college applications on the horizon, a demanding part-time job, and a bustling social life, Alex felt like they were constantly running on empty. The pressure to excel academically while maintaining a vibrant social media presence only added to their stress, leaving Alex feeling overwhelmed and disconnected from themselves.

One evening, after a particularly tiring day, Alex broke down during a conversation with their mother, Rita. Rita listened patiently before sharing her own experiences with managing stress during her teenage years. Rita introduced Alex to some mindfulness and relaxation techniques and emphasized the importance of self-care and setting healthy boundaries.

Inspired by Rita's advice, Alex decided to take proactive steps towards managing their stress and anxiety. They began by carving out time each morning to practice mindfulness. Sitting quietly in their room, Alex focused on their breathing, allowing themselves to be present in the moment, acknowledging their thoughts and feelings without judgment.

Journaling became a nightly ritual for Alex. They poured their thoughts, fears, and dreams onto the pages, finding clarity and a sense of release. This self-expression helped Alex understand their emotions more deeply and fostered a compassionate relationship with themselves.

Recognizing the importance of self-care, Alex began to set boundaries, both with themselves and others. They learned to say no to extra shifts at work and to social engagements that felt more draining than fulfilling. Alex communicated their needs to friends and family, who supported their decision to prioritize well-being.

Alex also sought support from a school counselor, who provided a safe space to explore their feelings and offered strategies for managing anxiety. This professional guidance was instrumental in helping Alex navigate their stressors more effectively.

As Alex implemented these changes, they noticed a profound shift in their mental and emotional state. The overwhelming waves of stress and anxiety began to recede, replaced by a sense of calm and self-assuredness. Alex discovered joy in simple pleasures, like reading for leisure and taking walks with their mother, activities that had fallen by the wayside amid their busy schedule.

Alex learned that managing stress and anxiety is not about eliminating challenges but about having a compassionate relationship with oneself. They realized the importance of listening to their body and prioritizing their well-being over academic or extracurricular demands.

Alex's story shows the power of vulnerability and taking steps towards self-discovery and healing. It highlights the importance of acknowledging stress and anxiety as part of the teenage experience and the transformative potential of self-care, mindfulness, and support in navigating this phase of life.

CHAPTER SUMMARY

- Teenage years are particularly prone to stress and anxiety due to changes, growth, and the quest for identity and independence.
- Stress and anxiety are natural responses to changes in life. Ways to manage them include acknowledging these feelings and finding supportive activities.
- Mindfulness and relaxation techniques, such as deep breathing, progressive muscle relaxation, visualization, and journaling, can help manage stress and anxiety.
- Self-care is essential in managing stress and anxiety. It involves recognizing your needs and taking steps to meet them, affirming your own self-worth.
- Setting healthy boundaries is crucial for protecting your mental, emotional, and physical well-being. It involves understanding and respecting personal limits.
- Seeking support, whether through friends, family, professionals, or support groups, is a step you can take to manage stress and anxiety.

CHAPTER 7
THE POWER OF RESILIENCE

R esilience is a word you might have heard quite a bit. But what does it truly mean, especially for you, a vibrant and evolving teen girl? Resilience is the remarkable ability to bounce back from challenges, setbacks, and failures. It's about facing a difficult situation head-on and emerging from it stronger and wiser than before.

Imagine resilience as a muscle in your heart and mind. It gets stronger every time you use it. Like any muscle, it requires practice, time, and care to develop. Life can sometimes throw curveballs your way. These could be anything from a bad grade on a test to a fallout with a friend or any other disappointment that life might present. In these moments, your resilience shines through, helping you navigate these situations with power and positivity.

Resilience is not about constantly feeling happy or never facing difficulties. It's about how you respond to and grow from these experiences. It's about acknowledging your feelings, learning from your mistakes, and moving forward with a positive attitude. This doesn't mean ignoring your emotions or pretending everything is okay when it's not. It's about giving yourself the time and space to feel, heal, learn, and step forward into your next chapter.

You already possess the ability to adapt and thrive. It's woven into your very being, waiting for moments to reveal its strength. And the beauty of resilience? It grows with you. Each challenge you face and overcome adds another layer to your resilience, making you even more capable of handling whatever life throws your way next.

So, whenever you face a new challenge, remember you are resilient. You have within you the power to overcome, learn, and grow.

HOW TO BUILD A RESILIENT MINDSET

Now, let's delve into how you can build a resilient mindset.

Building a resilient mindset isn't about shielding yourself from every hardship or pretending that challenges don't exist. It's about developing inner strength that helps you bounce back from tough experiences, no matter how hard it might seem. This mindset is the invisible armor that protects you, not by making you invulnerable but by empowering you to face life's battles with courage.

Your thoughts and beliefs about yourself play a significant role in resilience. If you constantly tell yourself you're not good enough or can't handle challenges, you're setting yourself up for failure. Instead, try to harness a compassionate inner voice. Speak to yourself with kindness and encouragement. This positive self-talk is a powerful tool in building resilience.

Another key aspect of a resilient mindset is embracing flexibility. Life is unpredictable, and sometimes, despite our best plans and efforts, things don't go our way. Instead of seeing this as a failure, view it as an opportunity to grow. Adaptability is a sign of resilience. It's about finding different paths to your goals and being open to new experiences and perspectives. It's okay to adjust your sails when the wind changes direction.

Resilience is closely tied to problem-solving skills. When faced with a challenge, a resilient person looks for solutions rather than dwelling on the problem. They break down overwhelming situations into manageable parts and tackle them one step at a time. This approach brings a sense of control and accomplishment and builds confidence in your ability to handle future obstacles.

Don't underestimate the power of a support network. Resilience doesn't mean going through tough times alone. It's about knowing when to seek help and lean on the people who care about you. Whether it's family, friends, or mentors, having a circle of support provides emotional strength and a sense of belonging.

Building a resilient mindset is a continuous process. It's about learning from every experience, embracing your vulnerabilities, and recognizing your inner strength. Remember, resilience isn't a trait that some people have and others don't; it's a skill that you can strengthen over time. Resilience is your key to overcoming obstacles and thriving when faced with adversity.

OVERCOMING OBSTACLES

You are bound to encounter obstacles throughout life. However, it's not the presence of these obstacles that defines you, but rather how you respond to them. Overcoming obstacles reflects our inner strength and resilience.

Imagine obstacles as mountains on your path. Some might be small hills, easy to climb with a little effort, while others might seem impossible to conquer, their peaks lost in the clouds. The size and nature of these mountains vary, but they all serve a purpose in your journey. They teach you patience, perseverance, and the importance of believing in yourself.

When faced with an obstacle, the first step is to acknowledge it. Denying its existence only gives it more power over you. Acknowledge it, but don't give it the power to define your abilities. You are so much more than the challenges you face.

Next, break down the obstacle into smaller, manageable parts. A mountain is climbed one step at a time. Identify the steps you can take to start your ascent. This approach makes the challenge seem less daunting and allows you to celebrate small wins along the way.

Climbing mountains is easier and more enjoyable with companions. Reach out to friends, family, or mentors who can offer support, guidance, or just a listening ear. There's strength in vulnerability, in admitting that you don't have all the answers and need help.

As you overcome each obstacle, take the time to reflect on the journey. What did you learn about yourself? How have you grown? These reflections help you build a resilient mindset and prepare for future challenges. With each obstacle you overcome, your confidence will grow, and what once seemed like insurmountable peaks will become just another part of the landscape of your journey.

Overcoming obstacles is about more than just reaching the other side; it's about the growth within you. Remember, the most beautiful views come after the most demanding climbs. Each obstacle you overcome is a step towards a more resilient and confident you.

LEARNING FROM FAILURE

Failure, as much as it is dreaded, is a powerful teacher. It's a hidden guide that, if listened to, can lead us to paths of unimaginable growth. This section will help you understand how you can learn from your failures to bounce back and leap forward with greater wisdom.

When we talk about failure, we must first change our perspective. Society often paints failure negatively as something to be avoided at all costs. However, the truth is that failure is a natural part of the learning process. It indicates that we are trying, pushing our boundaries, and daring to step out of our comfort zones. Every successful person you admire has faced failure. What sets them apart is their ability to learn from these experiences and not let them define their worth.

Learning from failure starts with accepting it. Acceptance doesn't mean you're okay with failing or don't strive for success. It means acknowledging that failure is a part of your growth journey. When you fail, allow yourself to feel the emotions that come with it—disappointment, frustration, sadness. It's okay to feel these emotions; they make you human. The key is not to dwell on them for too long. Allow yourself to process these feelings, and then, gently but firmly, shift your focus to learning.

Ask yourself, "What can I learn from this experience?" Every failure has a lesson hidden within it. It could be a skill you must develop, a different strategy you must try, or a reminder to be more patient and persistent. Reflecting on these lessons helps you grow stronger. It equips you with the knowledge and insight to face future challenges with a better strategy and mindset.

Sharing your experiences of failure and what you've learned from them can be incredibly empowering. It reminds us that we're not alone in our struggles and that failure is a universal experience. By sharing, we foster community and support, encouraging each other to keep progressing despite setbacks.

Learning from failure also means recognizing when to let go of a particular goal or path. Sometimes, despite our best efforts, things work out differently than we hoped. This doesn't mean you've failed; it means a different path is waiting for you, perhaps better suited to your strengths and passions. Being resilient means being flexible and open to new possibilities when we fail.

HOW TO STAY MOTIVATED

After embracing the lessons learned from failure, we can focus on maintaining a strong motivation. Much like a garden, motivation requires consistent care to flourish. It's the fuel that powers our journey through resilience, pushing us forward even when the path seems steep and unforgiving.

Motivation is not constant; it ebbs and flows like the tide.

There will be days when you feel unstoppable and others when even the simplest tasks seem difficult. This is perfectly normal. The key is not to let the low days define your journey or derail your progress. Instead, use them as moments of rest and reflection, a time to recharge and realign with yourself.

Setting small, achievable goals can help boost your motivation. When you break down your larger aspirations into manageable pieces, each accomplishment becomes a stepping stone toward your ultimate aim.

Another powerful tool for staying motivated is surrounding yourself with positivity. This includes supportive relationships that uplift you and distance yourself from negativity. Seek friends, family members, or mentors who believe in you and your dreams. Their support can be a beacon of light when your motivation falls.

Self-love is the key to staying motivated. Acknowledge your efforts and progress without harsh judgment. Understand that every journey has ups and downs; resilience is built when you respond to challenges.

Visualization can help you maintain motivation. Imagine your future self, having achieved your goals, basking in the glow of your accomplishments. Let this image be a source of inspiration, driving you forward through moments of doubt or hesitation.

Lastly, don't forget to find joy in the journey. Pursue activities that make you happy and fulfilled. Doing this ensures your motivation is fueled by a genuine love for what you do rather than what others want you to do.

CHAPTER SUMMARY

- Resilience is the ability to bounce back from challenges, setbacks, and failures. It's an essential part of personal growth.
- Resilience involves facing difficulties head-on, acknowledging feelings, learning from mistakes, and moving forward positively.
- Building a resilient mindset requires a compassionate inner voice, embracing flexibility, developing problem-solving skills, and having a support network you can rely on.
- Overcoming obstacles teaches us patience, perseverance, and self-belief, with each challenge faced adding to our resilience and confidence.
- Learning from failure is crucial for growth. It involves accepting failure, reflecting on lessons learned, sharing experiences, and being open to new paths.
- Staying motivated is vital to resilience. Setting achievable goals, surrounding yourself with positivity, practicing self-love, and finding joy in the journey can help you stay motivated.
- Resilience and motivation are not natural traits but skills that can be developed over time. They can contribute to a fulfilling journey of self-love and personal growth.

CHAPTER 8
EXPLORING SPIRITUALITY AND INNER PEACE

Spirituality invites you to explore who you are and connect with something greater than yourself. It's about finding meaning, purpose, and peace in your life. For some, spirituality is tied to religion, but it can also be experienced through nature, art, personal growth, and the relationships we form.

Spirituality is about discovering what truly matters to you. It's about understanding your inner world. It encourages you to listen to your heart, find solace in silence, and reach a sense of inner peace that can support you through life's ups and downs.

Spirituality also invites you to explore the beauty of the present moment, practice gratitude, and open your heart to the world's wonders. It's about finding joy in the simple things, learning to let go of what you cannot control, and focusing on what truly brings you peace and fulfillment.

For teen girls, exploring spirituality can be an empowering way to navigate the complexities of growing up. By engaging with your spiritual side, you can learn to appreciate your unique journey and discover a deeper part of yourself you didn't know existed.

There is no right or wrong way to explore your spirituality. It's a path that is unique to you. Whether you find solace in nature, are drawn to meditation and mindfulness, or find inspiration in creative expression, what matters most is that you are taking steps to connect with your inner self and the world around you.

When you explore your spirituality, you open the door to a world of inner peace, self-discovery, and unconditional self-love. It's a journey that will enrich your life and inspire those around you to explore their own paths to inner peace.

FINDING YOUR SPIRITUAL PATH

Discovering your spiritual path involves uncovering what resonates most deeply with you, your values, and your sense of purpose. It's about listening to your heart and allowing it to guide you toward practices and beliefs that bring you closer to your true self.

Finding your spiritual path takes time and an open mindset. It invites you to explore new traditions, practices, and beliefs you may not have considered before. One of the first steps in discovering your spiritual path is to reflect on what spirituality means to you. Consider what makes you feel most connected to something greater than yourself, whether through art, mindfulness, prayer, or acts of kindness. Think about moments when you feel alive, peaceful, and connected. These memories can offer valuable clues to your spiritual path.

Another aspect of finding your spiritual path is to create space for silence and introspection. In a world filled with constant noise and distraction, making time for quiet reflection can help you tune into your inner voice. This could be through yoga or meditation, spending time in nature, or simply sitting quietly with your thoughts. In these moments of stillness, you may find insights about yourself you never knew before.

Don't be afraid to seek out communities or mentors who can support you on your spiritual journey. Connecting with others who share your interests can provide valuable insights, encouragement, and a sense of belonging. Whether it's through online forums, local groups, or mentorship, being part of a community can enrich your spiritual exploration.

PRACTICES FOR INNER PEACE

The following activities can help you connect more deeply with yourself and bring you inner peace, especially if you're looking for an escape from the stresses of teenage life.

Meditation and Mindfulness

Meditation is a powerful tool for achieving inner peace. It allows you to pause, breathe, and connect with the present moment. As a teen girl, your life is filled with changes, challenges, and a constant search for identity. Meditation offers an escape from the noise, where you can listen to your inner voice without judgment. Start with just a few minutes a day, focusing on your breath or a mantra that speaks to you. You can extend this mindfulness to your daily activities, learning to approach life with a sense of calm and presence.

Journaling

Writing down your thoughts and feelings can be very therapeutic. It's a way to express yourself freely and reflect on your experiences. Journaling can help you understand your emotions, celebrate achievements, and learn from your struggles. It's a practice of self-love, acknowledging your journey, and recognizing your worth. You can start by writing about your day, things you're grateful for, or anything on your mind.

Creative Expression

Creativity is a beautiful way to explore your inner world and feelings. Whether through painting, drawing, writing poetry, or playing music, creative activities allow you to channel your emotions in a positive way. They can be a source of joy, relaxation, and a deeper connection with yourself. Don't worry about the outcome; focus on the process and how it makes you feel.

Connecting with Your Body

Your body is your home, and taking care of it is a form of self-love. Practices like yoga, dance, or walking with your pet can help you connect with your body and appreciate its strength and beauty. These activities improve your physical health and mental and emotional well-being. They teach you to listen to your body, honor its needs, and be kind to it.

Spending Time in Silence

Finding moments of silence can be incredibly refreshing in a world that's always buzzing with activity. Silence allows you to turn inward, away from the distractions of the outside world. It's an opportunity to be with yourself, reflect, and find peace. You can spend time in silence by sitting quietly in your room, walking alone, or simply pausing to breathe deeply throughout the day.

These practices are not one-size-fits-all. They are paths for you to explore and find what resonates with you. Approach them with an open mind, allowing yourself to grow and flourish uniquely.

THE ROLE OF NATURE AND SOLITUDE

Did you know that embracing nature and solitude can help you feel more connected to yourself and the world?

Nature offers a unique sense of peace and grounding. It's a reminder of the world's beauty and complexity and how you are a part of this magnificent world. Spending time in nature allows you to step away from the hustle and bustle of daily life, providing a space for reflection and connection with yourself on a deeper level. Whether it's a quiet walk through a park, a moment by the sea, or simply sitting under a tree, these natural experiences can help you feel more connected to the world.

Solitude offers a different kind of peace. In those quiet moments alone, you can genuinely listen to your inner voice, away from the outside world's influence. Solitude provides the space to reflect on your thoughts, feelings, and experiences. It allows you to understand yourself better. It's an opportunity to practice self-care, meditate, read, or simply be with your thoughts.

Combining the healing power of nature with the reflective quality of solitude can change your mental health. It allows you to find peace within yourself and the world, fostering a deeper connection to your inner self.

CONNECTING WITH A HIGHER POWER

Some people find that connecting with a higher power can help them understand their place in the universe and find inner peace. This connection can appear in different ways, depending on your beliefs and experiences. It's about feeling a part of something greater than yourself, which can provide comfort and a sense of belonging.

Connecting with a higher power also involves listening—listening with your ears, heart, and soul. This can be through meditation, prayer, or simply sitting in silence, allowing yourself to feel the presence of something greater. In these moments of quiet and solitude, you can often find the most profound sense of connection and peace.

For many, spirituality is not about adhering strictly to the rituals and teachings of a religion, though it can be for some.

Instead, it's about building an intimate relationship with the essence of life, the universe, or a divine presence.

Discovering your spiritual path is a journey of exploration and reflection. It begins with asking yourself meaningful questions about the nature of existence, the purpose of your life, and the values and principles that guide you.

It's okay not to have all the answers. Spirituality is as much about the questions as it is about the answers. It's about being open to the mystery and wonder of life and learning to trust the journey, even when the destination is unclear.

As you explore your spirituality, you may find that it enriches your life unexpectedly. It can offer a sense of purpose, inspire compassion and empathy, and encourage you to live in alignment with your true self. It can also comfort you during difficult times, reminding you that you are never truly alone.

Embracing spirituality is a powerful step in your journey of self-love. It invites you to look inward and outward with curiosity, connect with the world in a more meaningful way, and find peace in knowing you are a part of something much larger than yourself.

CASE STUDY: ZOE'S QUEST FOR INNER PEACE AND SPIRITUAL CONNECTION

Zoe, a 16-year-old high school student, felt increasingly disconnected from herself and the world around her. Amidst the pressures of academics, social expectations, and life in general, Zoe struggled to find a sense of purpose. She often questioned the deeper meaning of life and her place within it, feeling a void that school and social activities couldn't fill.

One evening, while scrolling through her social media feeds, feeling particularly lost, Zoe stumbled upon a quote about the power of nature and solitude in finding one's true self. This made Zoe wonder how she could find her own inner peace. She decided to embark on a quest to explore her spiritual side and connect with something greater than herself.

Zoe began her journey by dedicating time each morning to sit silently before starting her day. She created a small sanctuary in her room where she could meditate, free from distractions. This mindfulness practice allowed Zoe to start her day with a sense of calm and presence, gradually teaching her the value of living in the moment.

Inspired by her newfound interest in meditation, Zoe sought natural spaces to practice mindfulness and connect with the environment. She started taking long walks in her local park, where she paid close attention to the beauty of the natural world—the sound of the wind rustling through the leaves, the warmth of the sun on her skin, and the peacefulness of the quiet surroundings. These moments in nature became a source of comfort and inspiration for Zoe. It helped her feel grounded and connected to the world in a way she hadn't experienced before.

Zoe also discovered the therapeutic power of journaling. She began writing about her thoughts, feelings, and insights gained during her meditation and nature walks. Journaling became a way for Zoe to process her emotions, celebrate her growth, and reflect on her spiritual journey. Through writing, Zoe started to understand her inner world better and find a sense of inner peace.

Through her exploration of spirituality, Zoe learned the importance of self-love, gratitude, and the beauty of the present moment. She discovered that inner peace comes from within and that connecting with something greater than herself provided a sense of purpose and fulfillment. Zoe's journey changed not just how she viewed the world but also how she saw herself. She realized that her quest for inner peace and spiritual connection was not about finding all the answers but about embracing the journey and trusting the path that unfolded before her.

Zoe's story shows the power of spirituality in finding inner peace and deeper meaning in life. It highlights how mindfulness and nature can help deepen your perception of yourself and the world.

CHAPTER SUMMARY

- Spirituality is a journey of finding meaning, purpose, and inner peace. It's not restricted to religion; it can also be experienced through nature, art, and personal growth.
- Spirituality involves discovering what matters most to you, understanding your inner world, and recognizing the interconnectedness of all things. It encourages you to listen to your heart and find solace in silence.
- Exploring spirituality can empower you to navigate growing up, build self-esteem and self-love, appreciate your unique journey, and embrace imperfections.
- Spirituality encourages living in the present, practicing gratitude, and opening your heart to the world's wonders.
- Finding your spiritual path is an experimental process where you can explore different traditions and practices to connect with your true self.
- Some practices for fostering inner peace include meditation, mindfulness, journaling, creative

expression, connecting with your body, and spending time in silence.
- Nature and solitude can impact your spiritual journey, offering peace, grounding, and space for introspection.
- Connecting with a higher power can help you find comfort, guidance, and a sense of belonging when you feel lost.

CHAPTER 9
SPEAKING UP

S peaking up goes beyond simply being honest with others. It's a way to be true to yourself and honor your feelings, experiences, and perspectives. It's about giving voice to your innermost thoughts and standing firm in your beliefs, even when it's challenging.

Using your voice isn't always easy. It requires courage, strength, and vulnerability. It means opening up about what matters to you, sharing your thoughts and feelings, and not just what you think others want to hear. It's about asserting your needs and desires and respectfully disagreeing when your values don't align with what's being presented.

Why is speaking up so important, especially as a teen girl? Because it's what builds authentic relationships—with yourself and others. When you are honest about who you are, you attract people who appreciate the real you, not just the version of yourself you think others want to see. This authenticity fosters deeper connections that are based on genuine understanding and acceptance.

Using your voice empowers you and reinforces your sense of self-worth and confidence. Each time you voice your thoughts, you affirm your right to have opinions and to take up space in the world. This act of self-affirmation is a powerful form of self-love, as it acknowledges the value of your experiences.

However, speaking your truth also means being prepared for the fact that not everyone will agree with you or support your perspective. And that's okay. Disagreement does not reduce the validity of your feelings or experiences. It reminds us that diversity of thought makes life rich and complex. Learning to navigate these differences is part of the process.

Your voice reflects your inner world, and using it wisely can lead to meaningful change. Your voice matters. Your experiences, thoughts, and feelings deserve to be heard. Speaking up is not just about vocalizing your inner world; it's an act of self-love that empowers you.

THE POWER OF NO

Using your voice is also about knowing when and how to assert your boundaries. This brings us to a simple yet powerful word: "No."

"No" is a complete sentence. It doesn't require justification, explanation, or apology. But for many of us, especially in our teenage years, saying no can be tricky. We worry about disappointing others, being perceived as rude, or missing out. However, embracing the power of "No" is essential for our mental health and self-respect.

When you say no to something that doesn't align with your values, drains your energy, or doesn't feel right, you are honoring your needs and priorities. It's a declaration that you understand and respect your limits. This act of self-care sends a powerful message to yourself and others about your self-worth.

Saying no can also open doors. When you decline commitments that don't serve you, you create space in your life for experiences, relationships, and opportunities that do. This space allows you to engage more fully with what truly matters and makes you happy.

Learning to say no with confidence is a skill that takes practice. Start small, with low-stakes situations, and gradually work your way up. Pay attention to how you feel when you assert your boundaries. It might be uncomfortable at first, but it will become more natural with time. Remember, your feelings and needs are valid. You have the right to protect your time, energy, and well-being.

As you become more comfortable with saying no, you'll find that your ability to advocate for yourself and others strengthens. You'll be better equipped to stand up for your beliefs, support causes that matter to you, and contribute to positive change. When it's aligned with your values, saying no is an act of courage and self-love.

Embracing the power of "No" is a transformative step in your journey toward self-love. As you continue to empower your voice, remember that every no opens the path to a yes that resonates more deeply with who you are and aspire to be.

ADVOCATING FOR YOURSELF AND OTHERS

Advocating means standing up for yourself and lending your voice to those who might not have the strength or platform to do so. It's about harnessing the power of your voice in a way that respects yourself and others.

Advocating for yourself starts with understanding your worth. It's okay to ask for what you need, whether it's support, space, or respect. Asserting yourself doesn't mean being selfish or demanding; it means being true to yourself and honoring your needs and boundaries.

When it comes to advocating for others, it's about empathy and action. It's seeing someone in a situation where they're not being heard or respected and choosing to stand with them. This could be as simple as supporting a friend going through a tough time or speaking out against injustice in your community. Advocacy is about using your voice for good, uplifting and supporting others, and creating a ripple effect of positive change.

Advocating for yourself and others isn't always easy. It requires courage and resilience, especially when faced with opposition or indifference. But remember, every time you choose to speak up, you're not only empowering yourself but also paving the way for others to do the same. It's about creating a culture of respect and kindness where everyone's voice matters.

As you continue to navigate the complexities of adolescence and beyond, remember that your voice is a powerful tool for change. Whether in personal relationships, within your school, or in the broader community, never underestimate the impact you can make. By advocating for yourself and others, you're contributing to a world where everyone is seen, heard, and valued. And that, in itself, is a beautiful act of self-love and empowerment.

PUBLIC SPEAKING AND COMMUNICATION SKILLS

One of the most transformative skills you can develop is the ability to communicate effectively and confidently in public settings. Public speaking and communication are not just about making speeches or presentations; they're about expressing your thoughts and beliefs in a way that impacts others. This skill is a powerful extension of advocating for yourself and others, allowing you to share your voice and impact the world.

Feeling nervous about public speaking is entirely normal. Even the most experienced speakers feel a flutter of nerves before stepping onto the stage. The key is not to eliminate these feelings but to learn to harness them as a source of energy and passion for your message.

First, let's focus on the basis of effective communication: authenticity. When you speak from a place of authenticity, your words carry more weight and sincerity. This means being true to yourself, your values, and your message. It's about showing up as the real you, not a version you think people want to see. When you are authentic, your audience can connect with you on a deeper level, making your message more impactful.

Clarity is the next pillar of effective public speaking. Clarity in communication means being concise and direct, ensuring your message is understood. This involves organizing your thoughts beforehand and choosing your words carefully. A clear message is powerful because it leaves little room for misunderstanding, allowing your audience to grasp your perspective fully.

Another vital aspect of public speaking is engaging your audience. This can be achieved through storytelling, asking rhetorical questions, or even incorporating humor where appropriate. Engagement is about creating a two-way communication stream, even if the audience isn't speaking back. It's about making them feel involved, valued, and considered.

Lastly, practice is paramount. Like any other skill, the more you practice public speaking, the more comfortable and confident you become. Start small by sharing your thoughts in a more intimate setting, like a family dinner or a discussion with friends. As your confidence grows, seek out larger platforms to share your voice. Every great speaker starts somewhere; every opportunity to speak is a step toward mastering this empowering skill.

As you continue to develop your public speaking and communication skills, remember that your voice can inspire change, advocate for justice, and connect with others. By embracing this power, you are empowering yourself and paving the way for others to find their voices.

LEAVING A LEGACY

Your legacy is the impact your voice can have on the world. Your voice is not just a tool for expressing thoughts or commanding attention; it's a powerful instrument for change. This section explores what it means to leave a legacy through the power of your voice and how you, as a young woman, can harness this to make a meaningful impact.

Leaving a legacy is about creating something that outlives you and continues to inspire, empower, and guide others even when you're not physically present. It's about using your voice to plant seeds of change and hope in those around you and those who will come after you. Your legacy is the mark you leave on the world, a reflection of the lives you've touched and the difference you've made.

Start by reflecting on the values and causes that are important to you. What issues spark a fire in your heart? Is it advocating for mental health awareness, fighting for gender equality, or championing environmental conservation? Identifying your passions is the first step towards using your voice in a way that aligns with your values.

Once you've pinpointed these areas of passion, consider the platforms through which you can amplify your voice. In today's digital age, there are countless ways to make your voice heard, from social media and blogging to community volunteering and public speaking events. Each platform offers a unique opportunity to reach different audiences.

Leaving a legacy is not just about the scale of your impact but also about the depth of it. It's about the personal connections you forge, the lives you touch in meaningful ways, and the inspiration you inspire others to find their voices.

You will need to embrace resilience and perseverance on this journey. You will face challenges and setbacks, but it's through these experiences that your voice will become even more impactful. Each obstacle is an opportunity to learn, grow, and refine your vision for the legacy you wish to leave.

By empowering your voice with purpose and passion, you're not just leaving a legacy but shaping the future. So, speak up, speak out, and let your voice be a beacon of change, hope, and empowerment for future generations.

CHAPTER SUMMARY

- Self-love involves learning to speak up and honoring your feelings, experiences, and perspectives.
- Speaking your truth requires courage and vulnerability and allows you to assert your needs and set boundaries.
- Authenticity in expressing yourself helps form deeper connections with others and reinforces your self-worth and confidence.
- Embracing the power of "No" is crucial for your mental health, self-respect, and personal growth.
- Advocating for yourself and others involves standing up for rights, beliefs, and needs and using your voice for positive change.
- Developing public speaking and communication skills empowers you and enhances your ability to express your thoughts and beliefs to others.
- You can use your voice to inspire, empower, and guide others, creating a lasting impact and legacy.

CHAPTER 10
NAVIGATING CHANGE

Change is as inevitable in life as the rising and setting of the sun. It's a constant companion, sometimes arriving as a gentle breeze and, at other times, as a turbulent storm.

Change is the process of becoming different. This might sound simple, but its impact on your life can be profound and far-reaching. It can affect your relationships, self-image, goals, and even dreams. But here's the thing: change also brings growth, learning, and self-discovery, especially during your teenage years.

Understanding change begins with acknowledging that it is a natural part of life. Just as the seasons shift in a never-ending cycle, so too do the phases of your life. Each transition you face is not just an end but a beginning, offering new opportunities for you to grow and explore who you are. Whether starting a new school, moving to a different city, or navigating friendships and relationships, each change teaches you to adapt and learn.

One of the most empowering steps you can take is to welcome change with an open heart and mind. This doesn't mean it's always easy, or you won't face moments of doubt and uncertainty. It's natural to feel a mix of emotions when confronted with change. You might feel excited about the new opportunities ahead and anxious about leaving the familiar behind. These feelings are a normal part of the process; acknowledging them is the first step toward moving forward.

Everyone experiences change, and seeking support from family, friends, or mentors is okay. Sharing your thoughts and feelings can help you process your emotions and gain insights from the experiences of others. Practicing self-care is crucial during times of change. Taking care of your physical, emotional, and mental well-being can help you stay grounded in the face of uncertainty.

Understanding change involves recognizing that you have the power to shape how you respond to it. While you might not have control over every aspect of a transition, you do have control over your attitude and actions. By approaching change with a positive mindset and a willingness to learn, you can turn challenges into opportunities for growth. How you choose to navigate these transitions can shape the person you become.

EMBRACING NEW BEGINNINGS

As we journey through the winding paths of adolescence, we encounter moments that feel like standing at the edge of a new horizon. These moments are full of potential but often accompanied by uncertainty. Embracing new beginnings is not just about stepping forward into the unknown; it's about recognizing the strength within ourselves that makes each step possible.

New beginnings can take many forms. It may be starting a new school year, forging a new friendship, or discovering a hobby that sets your soul alight. Each offers a unique opportunity to learn more about who you are and who you aspire to be. It's a time to listen to your heart and trust your ability to navigate the journey ahead.

New beginnings give you a chance to redefine yourself. You are not bound by past perceptions or limitations. Instead, you can explore different facets of your personality, experiment with new interests, and grow in ways you never thought possible. Remember, self-love is at the core of this exploration. It's about allowing yourself to try, fail, and try again while knowing that you are worthy of love with every change that comes your way.

It's natural to feel a mix of excitement and apprehension. Accept these feelings as signs that you are alive and only human. Lean into the support of friends, family, and mentors who can offer guidance and encouragement. And remember to be that source of support for others, too. Shared experiences can deepen connections and provide comfort during times of change.

Change doesn't happen overnight, and challenges and

setbacks often accompany growth. Be gentle with yourself and learn from every experience.

HOW TO DEAL WITH LOSS AND GRIEF

In our lives, we are bound to encounter moments that challenge our strength and test our ability to stand back up after being knocked down. Dealing with loss and grief is one of the most overwhelming experiences that can impact our well-being. It's a universal part of the human experience. Still, it can feel isolating, especially during our teenage years when every emotion is magnified.

Loss is not just about the death of a loved one. It can also mean the end of a friendship, changing family dynamics, moving away from a place we call home, or even losing a part of ourselves that we cherish.

Grief is our emotional response to loss. It can appear in various ways—sadness, anger, confusion, or even numbness. It's important to understand that all these feelings are normal. They are not signs of weakness but indicators of our love and connection for what we've lost.

During these times, self-love becomes more important than ever. It's about permitting yourself to feel whatever you're feeling without criticism. It's about recognizing the strength within you, even when you feel most vulnerable. Some days will be better than others, and that's okay.

Here are a few steps to help you navigate through loss and grief.

Allow Yourself to Feel

Trying to bottle up your emotions or pretending they don't exist can lead to more pain in the long run. Allow yourself time to grieve, cry, or simply sit with your feelings.

Express Your Emotions

Whether it's through journaling, art, music, or talking with someone you trust, find a way to express what you're going through. Expression can be a powerful tool for healing.

Seek Support

Remember, you don't have to go through this alone. Lean on friends, family, or a support group where you can share your feelings and experiences with others who understand what you're going through.

Take Care of Yourself

Grief can take a toll on your physical well-being. Try to maintain a routine that includes proper nutrition, sleep, and physical activity. It's not about perfection but making small choices that honor your body and mind.

Find Moments of Joy

It might feel impossible initially, but try to find moments of joy in your daily life. It could be something as simple as listening to music, spending time with friends, or playing with a pet. These moments are not about forgetting your loss but about finding a balance.

Remember and Honor

Find a way to remember and honor the person, relationship, or part of yourself that you've lost. This could be through a memory book, a personal ritual, or a creative project. Honoring your loss can be a step towards healing.

Surrounding ourselves with understanding and compassionate people can provide a safe space to navigate our emotions and gradually find our footing again. The goal is not to move on from our loss but to learn to live with it, allowing us to feel a sense of peace and ease.

THE ROLE OF SUPPORT SYSTEMS

Support systems are invaluable during your teenage years. As you navigate life's changes, whether related to school, relationships, or personal identity, the people around you - friends, family, mentors, and even communities - play a pivotal role in how you perceive and tackle these changes.

A support system is not just a safety net for when things go wrong; it's a network of people that fosters your growth, resilience, and self-esteem. It's about having people who lift you up during your lowest moments. These individuals provide a mirror to your inner world, reflecting the strength and beauty you may not always see in yourself.

Building these relationships requires effort and intention. It's about choosing to surround yourself with positivity and genuine care. This doesn't mean that every person in your life will always understand what you're going through. However, it's about having at least one person who truly listens to your thoughts and feelings without judgment.

As we've explored in earlier chapters, a support system can also mean seeking professional help when needed. There's strength in recognizing when you need guidance beyond what your immediate circle can provide. Therapists, counselors, and other mental health professionals can offer invaluable perspectives and tools to help you navigate your emotions and experiences.

The quality of your support system is far more important than the quantity. It's about depth, not breadth. Having a few close, meaningful relationships is more beneficial than having numerous superficial connections. These deep bonds provide a sense of security and belonging, essential ingredients for self-love and acceptance.

As you move forward, remember that leaning on others is okay. Independence is a valuable trait, but interdependence—the ability to be independent while also relying on and supporting others—is a strength. Life's transitions become more manageable when you have a support system to share your joys, sorrows, and everything in between.

LOOKING FORWARD WITH HOPE

As you journey through your teens, you'll find yourself at the crossroads of numerous transitions. These moments, filled with changes and challenges, can sometimes cloud your vision with uncertainty. As we move from understanding the importance of support systems, let's shift our focus towards looking forward with hope, an equally important aspect of navigating life's transitions.

Hope is not just a feeling. It's a choice to believe in the possibility of a brighter tomorrow despite the current circumstances. It's about holding onto the light, even when the night is dark. For you, as a teen girl learning to embrace self-love, hope can be your guiding star. It can help you see beyond the immediate hurdles and recognize the endless possibilities that lie ahead.

To cultivate hope, start by setting small, achievable goals for yourself. These goals don't have to be monumental; they just need to be meaningful to you. It could be improving a skill, making a new friend, or even learning to appreciate your own company more. Achieving these goals will boost your confidence and reinforce your belief in your ability to influence your future positively.

Another way to foster hope is to practice gratitude. When we're focused on what's going wrong, it's easy to overlook the good in our lives. Take a moment each day to reflect on things you're thankful for, no matter how small. This practice can shift your perspective, helping you see the light in the midst of darkness and encouraging a hopeful outlook.

Hope is also about resilience. It's about getting back up when life knocks you down and learning from each experience. Every challenge you face is an opportunity to grow stronger and wiser. Embrace these moments, not with fear, but with the courage to believe you have what it takes to overcome them.

Looking forward with hope is not about denying the difficulties of today. It's about believing in the promise of tomorrow. It's about seeing yourself for who you are now and who you can become. As you navigate life's transitions, let hope guide you toward a future filled with endless possibilities.

CHAPTER SUMMARY

- Change is a natural and inevitable part of life, affecting various aspects such as relationships, self-image, and goals. It also offers opportunities for growth and self-discovery.
- Try to embrace change with an open heart and mind, even though it may bring a mix of emotions like excitement and anxiety.
- Seeking support from family, friends, or mentors and practicing self-care can help you better navigate change
- You can shape your response to change by adopting a positive mindset and a willingness to learn. This attitude can turn challenges into opportunities for growth.
- New beginnings present opportunities to learn more about yourself, redefine your identity, and embrace self-love.
- Dealing with loss and grief is part of the human experience. It requires allowing yourself to feel, seeking support, and finding moments of joy.
- A solid support system, including friends, family, mentors, and professional help, plays a pivotal role in personal growth, resilience, and self-esteem during the transitions of your teenage years.
- Cultivating hope through setting small goals, practicing gratitude, and surrounding yourself with positivity can help you navigate life's challenges and look forward to a future filled with possibilities.

YOUR SELF-LOVE JOURNEY

As you stand at this moment, on the brink of the rest of your life, take a moment to pause and reflect on the ideas we've explored together in this book. The path to self-love and embracing your spark is not the same for everyone.

It's a deeply personal voyage that has seen you navigate the calm and the storm, learning and growing with every step.

Think back to the moments of doubt and uncertainty, when loving yourself felt like an impossible challenge. These times tested your resilience and ability to stand firm in the face of adversity. But you persevered, armed with the knowledge and the tools you've gathered along the way. Each challenge is an opportunity to learn more about yourself and understand your needs, desires, and the incredible strength within you.

Remember the moments of triumph and joy, the milestones that marked progress on your journey. These are the times when self-love feels like a natural state, when you can see your worth and value reflected in the world around you. These moments are just as crucial to your journey because they remind you what you're working towards—a life where self-love has a permanent place in your heart.

There may be setbacks, such as when you stumble or fall short of your expectations. But with each of these moments comes the opportunity to practice self-compassion and treat yourself with the same kindness and understanding you would offer to a close friend. This, too, is an essential component of self-love because it allows you to celebrate your imperfections and recognize that they do not define your worth.

The journey of self-love is an ongoing one. There will always be new challenges to face and new lessons to learn. But you are now equipped with amazing tools that foster self-awareness, self-compassion, and resilience. You understand that self-love is not a destination but a continuous path. It's a path you will walk with confidence, grace, and an unwavering belief in your worth.

As you move forward, carry with you the lessons of the past, the joy of the present, and the hope for the future. Remember that self-love is your birthright, a legacy that you will continue to build with each day. It is the light that guides you through the darkness, the anchor that holds you steady in the storm.

So, take a moment to celebrate yourself and all that you've achieved. You are a work in progress, a masterpiece unfolding with each new chapter of your life. As you continue on this journey, know that you are not alone. You are part of a community of strong, resilient individuals walking this path alongside you, each of us striving towards a world where self-love is not just a dream but a reality.

THE CONTINUOUS PATH OF SELF-LOVE

The path of self-love does not have a definitive end. It's a continuous journey, unfolding with each step, offering new lessons and challenges that help you grow.

Self-love is an evolving practice that requires patience, understanding, and, most importantly, kindness toward yourself. It's about acknowledging your worth and value, even when you feel less than perfect.

Remember, perfection is not the goal; growth is. Each day presents a new opportunity to practice self-love, make choices that reflect your worth, and treat yourself with the same compassion you offer others.

As you continue on this path, you'll find that self-love becomes the basis upon which you build your life. It influences the decisions you make, the relationships you form, and the dreams you pursue. It becomes a source of strength and confidence, empowering you to face challenges with the right attitude and strength.

Allow yourself to explore new passions, step outside your comfort zone, and embrace the person you are becoming.

INSPIRING OTHERS

Your experience has the power to light the way for others. Your narrative is unique and holds universal truths about the human experience. The moments of doubt, leaps of faith, quiet mornings spent in reflection, and joyful discoveries of self-worth are chapters in a story many are waiting to hear. When you open up about loving yourself, you permit others to do the same. You show them it's okay to be imperfect, struggle, and grow.

Imagine a world where every young girl knows her worth, where she understands that her value is not dependent on the opinions of others or the number on a scale. By sharing your story, you contribute to this vision. You become a part of a larger narrative of empowerment and self-acceptance. Your voice, experiences, and insights become part of the collective wisdom that guides the next generation toward a kinder, more compassionate relationship with themselves.

Be authentic and honest when sharing your story. The most powerful stories are those told from the heart, without ego or embellishment. Your vulnerability is your strength. It connects you to others in profound and meaningful ways. It reminds us all that we all struggle or search for love and acceptance.

Your story can comfort someone who feels isolated in their experiences. It can challenge societal norms that dictate how we should look, think, or feel. Most importantly, it can inspire others to begin their own journeys of self-love and love themselves fully and unconditionally.

Your self-love legacy is not just about the relationship you've formed with yourself; it's also about how you use your journey to illuminate the paths of others. It's a legacy of kindness, courage, and connection—a reminder that we are all beautifully flawed, infinitely valuable, and deeply connected in our shared human experience.

COMMITTING TO LIFELONG GROWTH

Self-love is about embracing every part of who you are at every stage of your life and recognizing that growth is not only possible but essential.

Committing to lifelong growth means recognizing that the person you are today is not the final version of yourself. It's about permitting yourself to evolve, make mistakes, and learn from them. It's about understanding that every experience, whether good or bad, is an opportunity for growth and self-discovery.

This commitment can be challenging. It requires courage, resilience, and an unwavering belief in yourself. It means stepping out of your comfort zone, challenging your beliefs, and embracing the unknown with open arms. Within you lies an infinite well of strength and wisdom. You can overcome any obstacle, reach any height, and become the person you were always meant to be.

A FINAL MESSAGE

As we draw the curtains on this journey together, I want to leave you with a final message that I hope will resonate with you for years to come. This message is one of love and empowerment.

You are a work in progress. Every experience, lesson you've learned, and step towards loving yourself more deeply has added another stroke of beauty to your canvas.

As you move through life, know that the path to self-love will have ups and downs. There will be days when loving yourself feels effortless and days when it feels like the hardest thing in the world. On those tough days, I want you to remember this: You are not alone. You are part of a community of incredible women who are all on their own journeys of self-discovery and self-love. Lean on this community, share your stories, and let the strength of others lift you up when you need it most.

I also want to remind you that self-love is a radical act of empowerment. Choosing to love yourself just as you are is a powerful statement in a world that often tries to dictate how we should look, think, and feel. It's a declaration that you are enough, worthy of love and respect and have the right to take up space in this world.

So, as you close this book and step back into your life, I encourage you to carry these messages with you. Let them be your guiding light as you continue to grow, evolve, and become the most authentic version of yourself.

Remember, this is just the beginning of your self-love journey. And I am confident that you will create a beautiful, empowering legacy of self-love that will inspire others for generations to come.

Thank you for allowing me to be a part of your journey. Here's to your self-love legacy—a legacy that is uniquely and wonderfully yours.

YOUR FEEDBACK MATTERS

As we reach the end of this book, I extend my heartfelt gratitude for your time and engagement. It's been an honor to share this journey with you, and I hope it has been as enriching for you as it has been for me.

Your feedback helps me as an independent author and guides fellow readers searching for their next meaningful read. Your insights and reflections are invaluable; by sharing them, you contribute to a larger conversation that extends far beyond the pages of this book.

If the ideas we've explored have sparked new thoughts, inspired change, or provided comfort, I'd really appreciate it if you could share your experience with others by leaving a review on the platform on which you purchased this book.

Thank you once again for your company on this literary adventure. May the insights you've gained stay with you, and may your quest for knowledge be ever-fulfilling.

ABOUT THE AUTHOR

Ella Bradley is an educator and author, specializing in the development and empowerment of teenagers. With a rich background in child and teenager education, Ella has dedicated her career to equipping young minds with the knowledge and skills they need to navigate life successfully.

Her passion for education extends beyond the classroom and into her writing, where she addresses critical topics such as personal finance, career planning, and mental health. Ella's books are renowned for their practicality, clarity, and engaging style, making complex concepts accessible and enjoyable for teenagers.

Through her insightful and comprehensive books, Ella has helped countless teenagers take control of their futures. Whether she's teaching in a classroom or writing a book, her goal remains the same: to help teenagers grow into confident, capable adults.